D1491560

THE MASTER GARDENER'S GUIDE TO

GREEN HOUSE

GARDENING

A practical guide to growing under glass

ANN BONAR

SELECT
EDITIONS

A SALAMANDER BOOK

©1986 Salamander Books Ltd.

This edition published 1991 by
Selectabook Ltd.,
Folly Road,
Roundway,
Devizes,
Wiltshire, U.K.
SN10 2HR.

ISBN 0 86101 164 3

Credits
Editor: Jonathan Elphick
Designer: Kathy Gummer
Colour reproductions:
Rodney Howe Ltd.

Filmset: Modern Text Ltd.
Printed in Belgium by
Henri Proost & Cie,
Turnhout.

AUTHOR

Ann Bonar has been a horticultural writer and consultant for more than 20 years, and has written many books on various aspects of gardening. She is a regular contributor to a variety of gardening periodicals and trade journals, and has taken part in a number of gardening programmes broadcast by the BBC. For 12 years she has answered readers' queries sent in to a leading British weekly gardening magazine.

CONTENTS

Introduction

Protected gardening can be the entry to a dream world, a kind of tropical paradise, lush with dazzling flowers and exotic fruits and vegetables. It can be a place where plants grow to their full potential; rarely possible outdoors, even in their native climates. For the price of a little time and money, you can grow plants with the most perfect forms and colours.

SAVING MONEY AND TIME

There really is no need to spend a great deal of money in buying, for instance, the longlasting flowers of achimenes or streptocarpus, the superb velvety blooms of gloxinias or the glowing colours of begonias. Nor need time be spent on their care beyond planting and a few minutes a week on watering and tidying. Sweet peppers, which have one of the highest vitamin C contents of any fruit or vegetable, can be cropped to excess without artificial heat, training, or hand pollination. The initial sowing, potting and routine watering are all that is necessary. During the entire season, possibly two hours of your time may be spent picking sufficient fruit for an average family. It may be eaten immediately or put in the freezer.

Gardening is a hobby, and growing under glass is simply protected gardening. As with any hobby, how much time and money you spend on it depends, to some extent, on how enthusiastic you are about it. There are always other demands on your freedom and purse, both of which are finite.

A range of about 100 mixed ornamental plants can take 20 to 30 minutes to water each day

in the hottest part of summer, and you will need about half an hour a week for grooming and training. The spring routine of repotting, potting-on and general resuscitation for this number of plants can take two to three days, depending on the size of them.

If you increase plants yourself, from seed, bulb, tuber, division or cuttings, initially it should take one or two days for 100 plants. The young plants and seedlings will need daily attention for six to eight weeks, though this may be a case of merely looking at them on some days, to ensure that all is well. Increasing your own stock can cut costs by a considerable amount, and you have the satisfaction of knowing for certain that their roots are free from root pests.

However, starting plants from scratch needs some experience, and buying them in ready-made saves time and gives an immediate and attractive show.

PLANT PROTECTION

One of the biggest advantages of any type of greenhouse is its control of the growing environment, and especially the protection it gives from rain and wind. Damage from cold and even frost becomes a thing of the past with temperature regulated by artificial heating and control of the air supply. Diseases due to nutritional deficiencies are dispensed with at a stroke by using modern sowing and potting composts, which are the end-product of intensive research. Drought or flooding is no longer a problem, and predators and parasites can be controlled. A greenhouse, in fact, can be the plant equivalent of the most enlightened form of zoo where, although the animals are kept captive, the conditions are such that they refuse to leave when freed.

SITING YOUR GREENHOUSE

A free-standing greenhouse should be sited on level ground, away from any shade, preferably with a north-south facing aspect and close to a standpipe, the mains electricity supply and the garden shed.

Below: *Your choice of a site for the greenhouse should ensure that it is not shaded by trees or buildings, is sheltered from wind, and near the house. Access to mains water and electricity is important. If possible, site it to blend with the garden layout.*

Setting Up A Greenhouse

Greenhouses are available in many shapes and sizes, ranging from tiny lean-to's for patios to the grand conservatories-cum-living rooms. The dimensions of a standard greenhouse are about 8ft x 6ft (2·4m x 1·8m), with 7ft (2·1m) to the ridge, but a slightly larger one. say 10ft x 8ft (3m x 2·4m), will make a considerable difference to the kind and quantity of plants you can grow.

Above: *The ridged roof of this greenhouse allows plants to receive light of the same quality and quantity, whichever side they are, while the sliding door allows more precise control of ventilation than one on hinges, and takes up less space.*

AN OPTIMUM SIZE

The smaller the greenhouse, the more extreme the temperature changes will be, and at the height of summer, the daytime warmth may be excessive. For easier temperature and ventilation control a 12ft x 8ft (3·6m x 2·4m) greenhouse is probably the optimum size. This allows plenty of leeway for plant and crop experimentation, without too much expense in terms of heating and upkeep. The same considerations apply to lean-to's and conservatories, though they are modified by their use as living-rooms.

SPAN-ROOF GREENHOUSES

The span-roof greenhouse has a central ridge to the roof with equally-sized falls on each side. It stands free and may be glazed down to the ground. If so, it will absorb the maximum light but lose a good deal of heat in winter. Alternatively, the sides may be half-glazed, with the lower half consisting of a brick or wooden wall.

LEAN-TO'S

The lean-to is perhaps the next most popular type, either with a single sloping roof or as a three-quarter span lean-to, where part of the second slope of the roof has been retained. A disadvantage of the latter is that the back fall is difficult to clean and rapidly collects leaves in autumn. Similar plants to those of the span-roof can be grown in both, but the aspect can be much more limiting, as the temperature and light vary considerably according to which way the lean-to faces. A north aspect will ensure the well-being of ferns and foliage plants, whereas a south face will favour pelargoniums, cacti and tropical annual and herbs. An east-facing aspect receives very little direct sun after midday, but remains very warm. A west face, like a south face, can become too hot in the afternoon and early evening for many plants, unless they are watered two or three times a day and misted frequently. Three-quarter span greenhouses are slightly less hot.

MINIATURE LEAN-TO'S

The miniature lean-to's are only about 60in (150cm) high, the same in length and about 24in (60cm) deep. They are more like large frames stood on end than greenhouses, but they are ingeniously constructed to make the maximum use of interior space. They are therefore ideal for patios, basement areas or balconies. They provide adequate winter protection and generally earn their keep many times over, enabling you to grow tender crops like tomatoes or melons.

CONSERVATORIES

Conservatories serve a dual purpose as plant houses and living-rooms, and can easily be heated from the home central heating system. The cost of a custom-built Victorian replica can run into thousands of pounds, but the modern lean-to conservatory is just as elegant in design, easier to keep clean, better lit, and considerably less expensive.

PLASTIC GREENHOUSES

Plastic greenhouses have a considerable following and for cost-effectiveness the walk-in tunnel is probably the best. They consist of a series of giant metal hoops over which heavy-gauge clear or opaque plastic sheeting is stretched, and secured at ground-level. However, two to three years is the maximum life for this sheeting. It then discolours and perishes, due to the action of ultra-violet light.

FRAMEWORK AND FLOORING

Greenhouses made of glass need a strong, rigid support or framework for the glass, but in the interests of light transmission, the glazing bars should be as narrow as possible.

TIMBER FRAMEWORKS

Timber was the first material used for 17th-century portable frames, and until recently it was still the only one available. Although oak and teak are excellent and longlasting, they are extremely expensive. Western red cedar is also very durable and less expensive. It does not need painting, though you should apply linseed oil at intervals, and use brass screws and galvanized nails.

Baltic redwood, otherwise known as yellow deal or red deal, comes from the Scots pine and is commonly used for greenhouse frameworks, but is not very resistant to decay nor is it longlasting, so it must be painted regularly as well as being treated with a good preservative in advance. The cheaper wooden-framed greenhouses will contain less wood in their construction. They are therefore less strong and less capable of supporting heavy crops or full hanging baskets.

ALUMINIUM FRAMEWORKS

An aluminium alloy framework can be much narrower in section than a wooden one. It needs no maintenance and does not supply crevices for insects to hide or hibernate. However, considerable temperature fluctuations result in corresponding expansions and contractions. In badly-designed greenhouses this can result in gaps appearing between the glass and the framework during severe frost, and cracking glass in heat-waves. Screws, hooks and nails cannot be driven into it, so that supporting plants, hanging shelves, thermometers

Above: *An aluminium alloy framework needs no upkeep and ensures maximum light. It does not harbour pests and diseases.*

and other equipment can be a problem. However, many manufacturers do now incorporate drilled holes in the structure at suitable points to allow for wiring and bolts, and insulation kits supply special fittings for attaching the insulating sheet to the greenhouse interior.

CONCRETE

Reinforced concrete was used in greenhouse construction at a time when there was a shortage of wood. There may still be a few in existence today, but it is no longer in general use. Although it requires no upkeep, is virtually everlasting and extremely stable, it has to be wide in cross-section and thus decreases the availability of light. Visually, it is cumbersome and heavy, even when designed as a kind of Gothic arch.

SYNTHETIC ALTERNATIVES

Synthetic materials are now being tried, one of which has died a lamentably early death, though it appeared to be ideal. It consisted of structural grade polypropylene, injection-moulded and reinforced with glass-fibre. It was tough, strong, lightweight and waterproof. It needed no upkeep and could easily be washed down. However, others are sure to follow as research in this field develops.

PLANT SUPPORTS

Plants growing in glasshouse soil can be supported by stakes or canes or attached to the framework by wires, fillis (horti-cultural string) or twine. Plants in pots or other containers can be supported by split Chinese bamboo canes of various lengths.

Metal rings or 'cup' stakes will bear the weight of heavy flowers, just behind the petals. If wire is used it should be 12 to 14 gauge galvanized straining wire. This threads through galvanized wrought-iron 'eyes' anchored to terminal holdfasts. If an aluminium structure is involved, you will be dependent on ready-made holes in the structure for these fixtures.

FLOORING

The floor of the greenhouse can consist of indigenous garden soil or it can be concrete. A central concrete path or, if there is room, two such paths, with soil bordering each side, is ideal. Conservatories and lean-to's will have a solid floor, usually tiled. A concrete path leading to a free-standing greenhouse will be convenient, especially in winter.

Below: *In this attractive curved aluminium-framed greenhouse, maximum use has been made of space, taking into account the* different needs of the plants. *Some are supported by canes, others are held up by twine attached to the cross-bars.*

Tropical and subtropical plants must have some form of enclosed protection if they are to grow in a temperate climate, and green plants need light to photo-synthesize. A light-transmitting material is therefore necessary in any greenhouse construction.

Two thousand years ago the Romans used sheets of mica in frames to protect their plants. Until recently glass was the preferred material, but during the last decade synthetic glazing has been found satisfactory, and has become very popular.

GLASS

Horticultural glass must be free of air bubbles. Its standard weight, of 24oz per sq ft (672g per 30sq cm), helps to anchor a greenhouse. In the best green-houses, pane width is 24in (60cm), but frequently panes are only 18in (45cm) wide by 20in (50cm) long. Note that they should overlap, not be butted. The light transmission of glass is about 90% of the natural source of light but unless it is kept clean, it will drop considerably. The length of life is indefinite, or as long as it takes you to break it!

Unfortunately glass is a good conductor of heat, so that warmth inside the greenhouse is absorbed by the interior of the glass and then rapidly transferred to the outer surface, where it radiates into the air. If the outside air is already warm but calm, the speed of conduction will be slow or non-existent, but cold outer air will considerably increase the rate, as will windy conditions, and the two together are very dangerous to tender plants (see also pp. 18-19).

Glass is a brittle material, easily shattered and capable of causing lethal wounds. It must be handled carefully and, if cracks appear in panes, they must be sealed at once to prevent draughts, further shattering and breakage of the entire pane.

Top: *A wooden-framed greenhouse maintains a steady temperature level. The glazing is bedded into putty.*

HOW TO SECURE GLASS

Glass is generally kept in place with putty, or putty substitutes. For greenhouses with metal frameworks, the alloy surface has to be specially prepared and the putty may be different to that used for timber sashes. Many glasshouse manufacturers have developed systems of securing the glazing with spring clips or synthetic moulded beddings. Whatever system is used, it must provide a watertight and airtight seal between glazing and structure, regardless of tempera-ture and without causing the glass to crack.

Above left: *The glass in a metal-framed greenhouse is secured by metal spring clips, which are easy to fit.*

Above: *The latest greenhouses are made of shatterproof and mouldable polycarbonate, with glass for the lower panels.*

SYNTHETIC GLAZING MATERIALS

As the potential of plastic materials is being realised synthetic substitutes are coming on to the market. It is now possible to buy a clear, bullet-proof sheet called polycarbonate. At a thickness of ⅛in (3mm), it weighs 23oz per 39sq in (650g per sq m), which is approximately a third of the weight of glass. Its lifetime is indefinite from the point of view of toughness but, while light transmission is initially 83%, after about 12-15 years it will deteriorate, and the material itself breaks down.

Acrylic is also being used to produce a glass-like material $\frac{1}{10}$in (2mm) thick which, while not as strong as polycarbonate, and therefore not as expensive, has similar light transmission and ageing properties.

Like glass, both these synthetic materials are mouldable, and polycarbonate in particular has been used in the design of greenhouses with curved frameworks.

Whether you have glass or synthetic glazing in your green-house you must keep it absolutely clean, especially in urban areas, and take care to avoid scratching synthetic glazing.

It is possible to grow a much greater variety of plants in an unheated greenhouse (a cold-house) than outdoors. In severe winters it will not always prevent plants from being frosted, but it does ensure that they will flower earlier in spring, and later in autumn. It means that many of the hardiest can flower in late winter when they would normally be dormant, and it enables sub-tropical crops and ornamentals to be grown in summer.

COOL-HOUSES

If you heat the glasshouse so that the temperature never drops below 45°F (7°C), you are creating what are known as 'cool-house' conditions. It then becomes feasible to grow an even wider variety of plants. Nor are you so dependent on the seasons. Summer crops can be harvested at least a month earlier than outdoors because they can be started so much earlier. Lettuce can be grown throughout the winter and chrysanthemums last until mid-winter. You can crop strawberries in mid-spring, and primulas, cinerarias, calceolarias and freesias will flower in winter. For spring salads you can grow beet, onions and French beans (see pp. 68-71 for lists of plants to grow in cold and cool-houses).

Glasshouses can be heated with paraffin, electricity, gas, solid-fuel or oil.

PARAFFIN HEATERS

Paraffin stoves are the simplest and cheapest method of heating small greenhouses. Models are now made specifically for glass-house work. Single or double burners, of different sizes, radiate heat according to the rate at which the wicks burn. Some have hot-water pipes attached, so that warmth is given off along the pipes and from the exhaust at the ends. Good quality paraffin

is virtually free from impurities and, provided the wick is kept absolutely clean and is accurately trimmed, it will not damage plants. While burning, oxygen is used up and carbon dioxide given off, so ventilation is essential, except with one model, which has a flue fitted. Remember that with every gallon of paraffin burnt a gallon of water is produced.

ELECTRIC HEATING

Electric immersion heaters with a thermostat can be used to heat hot-water pipes. Banks of tubes, usually located beneath the staging, and panel heaters are also available for glasshouses, as are fan-heaters and convector heaters. The latter two cost slightly less to run.

Below: *Paraffin heaters are portable, easy to run and give out appreciable warmth for little expense. A flue pipe helps heat distribution, but is not essential. Ensure that the heater is designed for greenhouse use.*

Above: *A control panel is useful, enabling you to control all your equipment thermostatically from one site. Make sure it has fused, switched sockets.*

GAS HEATING

There are few manufacturers today who produce gas heaters. Although initially expensive, they are economical to run.

SOLID FUEL HEATERS

Most of the heaters mentioned so far are suitable for small greenhouses, either because of cost, or size. Solid fuel boilers rely on hotwater pipes, which can be used in any size of greenhouse. The modern boilers are designed for easy installation and running. They are suitable for virtually any type of solid fuel, not just anthracite or coke. Boilers can also be run on gas or oil, though oil is unsuitable for small greenhouses, except where the domestic central-heating is run on oil and the greenhouse is attached to the home. Then it should be possible to run a radiator off from the house.

CALCULATING AND CONSERVING HEAT

The calculation of the total amount of heat lost from a glasshouse is important, since it dictates the size of the heating apparatus and affects the setting of a thermostat. It depends on many factors, such as the area, in square feet, of all the materials used in the structure, including the glass, its size and design, and the heat lost from leakages and ventilation.

HOW TO CALCULATE HEAT LOSS

Heat transmission coefficients for brickwork (plastered or otherwise) concrete, aluminium and all other materials must be included in the calculation. The difference between the lowest possible outside temperature and the one that should be maintained in your greenhouse gives the temperature lift in degrees.

Each area of material must be multiplied by its appropriate coefficient, the areas then added together, and another third of the total added to account for leakages. This sum is then multi-plied by the temperature lift. The result gives a figure in BTUs which represents the loss of heat that will need to be made up under the most extreme conditions. In practice nowhere near so much heat will have to be supplied most of the time.

If you wish to make your own calculations, a complete list of transmission coefficients can be obtained from the manufacturer. However, for a given size of greenhouse and temperature minimum there is generally a compatible size of heater. It is only where conditions are not average, as in cold areas or on exposed windy coasts, that changes will be necessary. In such cases, a heating engineer is in a much better position to determine the size of heater.

MAINTAINING HEAT

For the smallest areas of 10 x 6ft (3 x 1·8m) and 8 x 8ft (2·4m x 2·4m), a paraffin heater is sufficient to keep temperature well above freezing in all but the severest weather, though

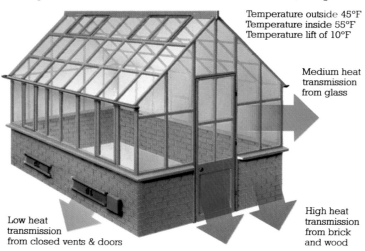

Temperature outside 45°F
Temperature inside 55°F
Temperature lift of 10°F

Medium heat transmission from glass

High heat transmission from brick and wood

Low heat transmission from closed vents & doors

Above: *Heat loss from a greenhouse depends on the materials of which it is made. To calculate the amount of heat required,* the coefficients of heat transmission for each need to be known. Natural leakage will account for further loss.

Above: *Various kinds of plastic insulation are available; this is bubble glazing, three sheets of plastic containing air pockets.*

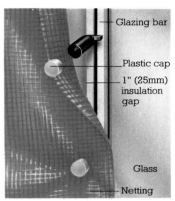

Glazing bar

Plastic cap

1" (25mm) insulation gap

Glass

Netting

Above: *Insulation can be attached to metal framework with special clips which allow a space between glass and insulation.*

temperature cannot be regulated by a thermostat: these are only applicable to electrical and gas-fired boilers.

Since glass is highly heat-permeable, it does little to protect plants from cold but its light-conducting qualities have always overridden this consideration. However, ways have been found of both supplying heat economically and containing it, without undue loss of light.

INSULATION

Extra protection for plants used to be supplied by a light covering of newspaper, muslin or netting at night and during the day if necessary. Now plastic materials are being used to insulate glass on the inside, forming a kind of double glazing. The simplest kind is a clear polythene sheet which prevents condensation by ensuring that moisture runs down the sides and drips on to the soil at ground level, rather than on to the plants from above.

Propylene/polyethylene netting is another good insulating material. It has ⅛in (3mm) mesh and it is cross-bonded for extra strength. It gives good ventilation,

little drip from condensation and provides shading in summer. Bubble-glazing, whether it has small ¼in (6mm) or large 1in (25mm) air bubbles, is an even more effective insulator. The small-bubble plastic sheeting consists of a double skin containing sealed air pockets; the large-bubble type is a 3-ply polythene film, the centre layer of which contains the sealed bubbles, so that both the outer surfaces are flat.

Sheets of corrugated rigid plastic, coloured, transparent or white, are available and can be cut easily, or you could buy polythene sheets reinforced with wire mesh. All these are attached to the inside of the greenhouse and sealed to leave a 1in (25mm) air space. Metal-framed greenhouses have special clips for these types of attachment (diagram above).

Greenhouses can be partitioned by using insulating materials as curtains, and heating one section only.

Double glazing with glass or polycarbonate is as practicable as it is with domestic glass, and some of the modern conservatories are sold with this as part of the package.

STAGING AND DISPLAY SHELVING

Standard staging consists of horizontal wooden slats supported by legs at about waist level. This is a good working and display height. The slats allow ventilation round the containers and free drainage of surplus moisture.

OTHER TYPES OF STAGING

Solid tops with a lip around the edge are useful for many jobs, such as potting, sowing and pricking out. The lip prevents compost falling to the ground. Another variation is the metal tray, which fits on to the top framework, and has either a solid base, or a wire or plastic netting base. The solid base can be filled with a shallow layer of water-absorbent aggregate, such as shingle, gravel, peat, grit, polyester capillary matting or clay granules which expand with great heat to form lightweight brown pebbles. If water is added to the tray, its gradual evaporation helps to keep the atmosphere moist, the plants cool and the roots damp, without being waterlogged.

While you can make your own wooden staging to suit your house and plant requirements, the aluminium kind can be obtained ready-made. One company produces this staging in units, which can be built up to form tiers and steps. The design is sufficiently neat and attractive to be used in conservatories or anywhere that plants are displayed.

Metal staging requires no upkeep, is lightweight, and easy to clean. Wooden staging

Below: *Slatted wooden staging can be used in tiers and allows good ventilation for plants; it encourages humidity and helps drainage of surplus water.*

provides a great many nooks and crannies for insect pests and fungal spores to hibernate or rest for the winter, so it must be thoroughly scrubbed down and sterilized every year. It can also decrease the quantity of light to an unacceptable degree.

Staging has to be strong, rigid and capable of bearing considerable weight. A lower tier near the soil for storage of resting plants, pots, compost, trays, and other paraphernalia is useful. Avoid staging with longitudinal bracing bars from end to end near the ground, as these make it very awkward to stand comfortably when working, and are a nuisance where storage is concerned.

Below: *Metal staging makes a good display unit, which can be added in sections, and is easily cleaned. Fill the trays with sand or capillary matting.*

Staging is not essential in a glasshouse, however, and may even be a drawback; for instance where plants are growing in the soil which makes up the greenhouse floor. However it is necessary to have some kind of working surface, and a good compromise is to erect staging down one side of the greenhouse and leave the other free.

SHELVING

Shelving is an optional extra. Solid or slatted kinds are available, but the latter allows water to drip on the plants beneath it. Since it is usually above the staging, near the roof, it reduces the amount of light reaching the plants, so position it carefully. Consideration must also be given to headroom requirements and extra roof strain. Some manufacturers supply houses fitted with shelving or with brackets for it.

GREENHOUSE EQUIPMENT

A greenhouse is an artificial environment for a plant. The atmosphere and the growing medium are quite different to its natural one, and its roots are more restricted. The plant therefore needs to be monitored closely. As you gain experience you can do this yourself, simply by looking and feeling, but in the meanwhile there are a variety of gadgets to do this for you. Even the experienced gardener finds these useful with the more temperamental plants, and some of the gadgets also save time, and ensure that jobs are done automatically.

THERMOMETERS

An essential monitor is the maximum and minimum thermometer, from which you can determine how low the temperature fell at night, as well as how high it rose in the daytime. This instrument often provides a clue as to why plants are growing too slowly, or not at all, are not ripening, or are subject to fungal diseases.

There are also thermometers that give a read-out of the soil temperature, which is an important factor in plant growth, especially when sowing seeds or putting in young plants.

A VARIETY OF METERS

Small, handy, inexpensive meters are now available which record the moisture content of the soil or compost, together with its pH value. Others measure the intensity of light reaching the plants, and a hygrometer will record the degree of humidity.

THERMOSTATS

A thermostat should be installed to regulate temperature in a greenhouse heated by either electricity or a boiler run on gas. It should normally be an air thermostat, but where an immersion heater is in use, a water thermostat is necessary. For air, the rod type is best. Be sure that it switches on at the same temperature as it is set to switch off. It must be waterproof and capable of working in a humid atmosphere, and it is wise to avoid buying the cheapest models, as these are likely to break down before long. Air thermostats should be screened

Below: *Equipment for monitoring or controlling the greenhouse environment: maximum and minimum thermometers, moisture meters for composts, and a rod thermostat for regulating warmth.*

Above: *Equipment includes, from left, clockwise: labels, aerosol insecticide, plastic measuring jugs, greenhouse twine (fillis), widger, dibber, split rings, measuring spoon, knife, secateurs.*

from direct sunlight and from rising hot air. They should be sited 8in (20cm) from the glass, well away from the door and the ridge.

VENTILATION EQUIPMENT

All greenhouses need ventilation. Some are fitted with automatically-opening vents, which are particularly useful on spring days when the temperature changes every five minutes, or when the greenhouse is left unattended all day. Ordinary ventilators can be converted quite easily. There are two types of automatic greenhouse ventilator. One is a stainless steel tube, containing a mineral wax, which expands with warmth. The other is a strong brass alloy spring, which also expands and contracts with changes in temperature. Both can be set to open between given temperatures.

OTHER EQUIPMENT

Other useful equipment includes scales, small graduated containers and spoons for measuring solutions, a tape-measure or ruler, a steel widger for lifting seedlings when pricking out, and if possible, a box measuring 22in x 10in x 10in (55cm x 25cm x 25cm), which will hold exactly 1 bushel (36·4 litres) of compost: John Innes composts are made up by the bushel. A 20in diameter sieve of ¼in (6mm) mesh and a shovel will also be necessary if compost is to be made up at home.

SPRAYERS

Some form of sprayer is essential: a small 1pt (½ litre) hand-held mister is useful, particularly in the conservatory. It can also be used for dispensing pesticides. If you need a larger one special syringes with coarse or fine jets are available. Sprayers of ½ gal (2·5 litres) capacity, which are pumped up before use, are useful for overhead spraying or pest and disease control in large greenhouses.

CONTAINERS

There are containers of all sizes and depths available, from tiny 1in (25mm) wide ones to the 3ft (90cm) tubs, made in a variety of materials, including plastic.

CLAY POTS

Formerly, plant pots were always made of terracotta-coloured clay, with diameters from 2in (5cm) up to 18in (45cm) and depths more or less the same, though the base was always narrower than the top by about a third. This was to make it easier to remove the root-ball from the pot, and to ensure that the roots were damaged as little as possible. Such pots had a single round drainage hole in the centre of the base.

Shallow pots were also made, called 'half pots', which were about half the depth of normal

Below: *Plant pots: terracotta-coloured clay, breakable and heavy but good for big plants; plastic, light, easy to clean, long-lasting; black plastic-sheet bags, throwaway; and rings of bituminized card for ring-culture.*

pots and with correspondingly wider bases. They were intended for seed-sowing, for plants with small root systems in proportion to their top growth, or for plants needing more drainage material than usual. Pots of greater depth, known as 'Long Toms', could also be obtained, and these were meant for plants with long tap-roots, such as sweetpeas or certain kinds of alpine plant.

Clay pots are comparatively heavy, and can be broken. Chemicals from hard water and fertilizer solutions become deposited in them as white bands and markings, and these impede the drainage and aeration of the clay, as well as being harmful to the plant's roots. However, with care and regular cleaning they will last indefinitely. They keep roots cool and, because clay is moisture-absorbent it acts as a buffer, and prevents rapid drying-out. They have great aesthetic quality, particularly the Provençal and Italian planters.

PLASTIC POTS

There is a wider range of sizes, shapes and colours in the newer

plastic pots. Although they are almost exact copies of the clay ones, they are much thinner and lighter in weight, and they have several drainage holes, because plastic is hardly permeable. They do not break if dropped but can be cracked if flattened, and will eventually deteriorate and become brittle. They are easily cleaned and freed from debris, pests and diseased material, and do not accumulate salt deposits. They are convenient and economical to use, and are well-suited to soilless composts of peat and sand, which contain no loam. Such composts do however have a tendency to dry out within a few hours in these pots. Compost in clay pots dries slower.

Plastic pots are easy to obtain and are stocked by all garden

Above: *Other plant containers include troughs for a group of plants, hanging baskets of green plastic-covered wire, hung from a securely-attached bar, and wall pots on the framework.*

centres and shops. The cost is about half that of the clay pots, which are not always available now. For both clay and plastic pots, you can buy saucers to fit the various sizes.

TROUGHS AND TUBS

For large plants, groups of plants, and specialist displays there are other types of containers. You can obtain troughs from 2ft-5ft (60cm-150cm) which are made of wood, polypropylene, expanded polystyrene or fibreglass.

25

Some fibreglass troughs are moulded and coloured to look like Italian Renaissance lead troughs. They should all have drainage holes. Wooden ones must be treated with a wood preservative harmless to plants, whether they are painted afterwards or not.

Tubs are now also of plastic as well as wood, again in a variety of shapes, colours and sizes and different types of plastic.

HANGING BASKETS

Hanging baskets greatly enhance ornamental displays in conservatories and greenhouses. They can be made of plastic, wire or wood and may be 10in, 12in or 14in (25cm, 30cm or 38cm) wide. Plastic ones are longlasting, coloured green, brown or beige, lightweight and inexpensive. Soil or compost in wire mesh baskets dries out quickly, unless it is lined or a saucer is placed in the basket base. If the wire is covered with plastic mesh, it may not be galvanized, in which case its life will be short, particularly as full baskets are heavy. The wooden ones consist of thin woven strips; they are heavier, and must be treated annually with a preservative.

Above: *Hanging baskets make an extremely attractive feature, but must be well secured.*

GROW-BAGS

The popular grow-bag is a plastic sack filled with compost and laid flat on a floor to avoid using soil, which might be contaminated with disease or pests. Tomatoes, lettuce, aubergines, peppers and melons are just some of the crops which can be grown in these. They are also suitable for growing ornamental plants. Special supports for plants in grow-bags have been designed and are available.

PROPAGATING BOXES AND TRAYS

A great many propagated plants owe their early success to the protection of glass.

Shallow wooden boxes or plastic trays 1½in-3in (40mm-75mm) deep and about 14in x 9in (35cm x 23cm) are used for sowing seed. Wooden boxes rely on the small gap between the base boards for drainage, whereas plastic ones have holes pierced in the base at regular intervals. Cuttings can also be

Above: *Soil blocks for seed sowing can easily be made at home with a block-maker.*

rooted in these containers. For small quantities of seed there are half trays, and the half pots described earlier (see page 24).

INDIVIDUAL SEED CONTAINERS

When you want to sow seed very thinly, or when each seed is large or pelleted (contained in a hard ball-like shell which dissolves in the soil), you can use either small, individual containers or miniature cylindrical blocks of peat, known as Jiffy 7s. The latter are dry, compressed discs of peat about (½in) 15mm thick, held together on the outside with a skin of fine plastic netting. Before use leave them to soak in water. They will swell up to a size of about 1½in x 1¼in (40mm x 30mm), with a small indentation in the top. Remove the netting, if you wish, just before planting.

There are also peat blocks shaped like miniature pyramids, soil blocks, made of compressed compost, and small 2in (5cm) peat pots which absorb into the

soil or surrounding compost when planted out.

Always keep the soil or peat in these type of containers moist, as once the outside has dried out, it is difficult to wet it thoroughly again.

The merit of blocks, expanding discs and peat pots is that they can be planted out without disturbing the roots. They also enable the plant to grow to a reasonable size so that it is strong enough to withstand slug, snail and weather damage.

PROPAPACKS

Propapacks are an ingenious form of container. They consist of expanded polystyrene slabs with a series of open-ended pot-shaped cells. Compost is poured into the cells, and then firmed with the pegs of a compressor board. The seed is sown individually or one cutting is placed in each cell. When the seedlings are ready to plant, the compressor board is placed flat side down and the propapack on top, so that each cell is located with a peg on the board. As the propapack is pushed down each plantlet is pushed up, ready to plant without damage.

COMPOSTS AND OTHER GROWING MEDIA

Container plants cannot grow successfully in soil out of the average garden. There are all sorts of organisms, such as fungi, bacteria, insects, worms, and nematodes in the soil, and some of these will feed or live on plant roots. The drainage and aeration is inadequate for container plants, and often for garden plants too, and the plant food is likely to be deficient or incorrectly balanced.

PLANT NEEDS

The soil for plants grown in the confined space of a container has to be very carefully blended. As the roots do not have unlimited space in which to search out water and nutrients, both must be available at all times, in the correct quantity. The growing medium must therefore retain water but no so much that it becomes waterlogged and short of air. It must also contain nutrients, but not so much that the roots become poisoned by an excess of them.

JOHN INNES COMPOST

Professional head gardeners, working in Victorian glasshouse ranges, evolved their own recipes for composts. There were probably as many recipes as gardeners, but in the 1930s two research scientists at the John Innes Horticultural Institute in England (now part of Norwich University) produced some formulae for container soil, which could be standardized, and easily made up. These came to be known as the John Innes Seed and Potting Composts, and have been in regular and widespread use ever since. The formulae are as follows:

Seed compost 2 parts sterilized loam, 1 part peat, 1 part sand (all parts by volume), plus 1½oz (45g) superphosphate of lime and ¾oz (21g) of chalk per bushel (36·4 litres) of the mixture. Loam is soil that is an ideal blend of clay, silt, sand and humus, completely decomposed animal and plant matter.

Potting compost No 1 7 parts loam, 3 parts peat, 2 parts sand, plus 4oz (112g) Jl base fertilizer and ¾oz (21g) chalk per bushel (36·4 litre). The base fertilizer consists of: 2 parts hoof-and-horn, ⅛in (3mm) grist (13% nitrogen), 2 superphosphate of lime (18% phosphoric acid) and 1 sulphate of potash (48% sulphate of potash). All parts are by weight.

6mm sieve

½pt (0·2 litre) water
Bring water to boil

Sieved, dried loam
Boil for 7 mins.

Small amounts of soil can be steam-sterilized without special apparatus. Use a 6-pt (3·4 litre) saucepan and good loam, add the sieved loam to ½pt (0·2

litres) boiling water, bring back to the boil and boil for 7 minutes with the lid on. Remove and leave for 7 minutes more, then spread out.

Potting compost No 2 is the same except that the quantities of fertilizer and chalk are doubled, and in No 3 they are trebled. Acid potting compost for lime-hating plants, such as heathers and azaleas, is made by substituting flowers of sulphur for the chalk.

For good drainage use coarse sand, free from organic matter, shells, silt or clay. Sea sand is unsuitable. Remember to mix only when the sand is dry.

PEAT

The spongy quality of peat helps to keep a compost open and aerated, and at the same time regulates its moisture-holding capacity over a long period, as it decomposes slowly. For composts, a granulated form is preferable, with a pH of not less than 3·5. It is almost completely sterile, and free from weed seeds, pests and diseases, like sand. Peat should be moistened before mixing.

Peat has been greatly used in composts and the supply now begins to show signs of being finite. Substitutes for it have been tried, two of which are vermiculite and perlite.

VERMICULITE

Vermiculite is a silicate mica of volcanic origin, sometimes called 'fool's gold' because of its glittering iridescence. The particles, when heated to high temperatures, expand to between $\frac{1}{16}$in and $\frac{1}{4}$in (1·5mm and 6mm) in size, and they can hold more water and air than peat, as well as retaining warmth. After 3 to 4 years in the soil, they break down. Vermiculite's main use is for seed germination or for rooting cuttings, either alone or mixed with peat.

PERLITE

Perlite is also a volcanic silicate,

looking like glassy rock. Fast heating to high temperatures expands the particles into light-weight, rigid granules, which retain their volume over many years, and can be repeatedly used if sterilized. They also retain warmth, and can be used alone for rooting cuttings, or as a 50:50 mixture with peat for seeds and potting, with nutrients added.

LOAM

Besides acting as an anchor, loam contains actively decomposing humus. It therefore supplies nutrients but it can of course also contain pests, diseases and weed seeds. A suitable loam for these composts should be of a medium texture and weight. It should have a pH of approximately 6·0 to 6·5 and must never be chalky. Take care to sterilize before mixing.

Small quantities can be steri-lized in a 6pt (3·4 litre) saucepan. Sieve the loam though a $\frac{1}{4}$in (6mm) sieve and spread out to dry. Add a measured $\frac{1}{2}$pt (0·3 litre) of water to the saucepan and boil. Then fill with soil to within $\frac{1}{2}$in (15mm) of the rim. Put the lid on and boil for exactly 7 minutes. Then take it off the heat and leave to stand for 7 minutes with the lid on. Put on to a clean surface to cool, and store in a clean container. Do not allow it to become dry before use. For large quantities, proprietary sterilizers can be obtained. If you do not adhere strictly to the times and quantities specified for sterilizing loam you will obtain poor results, and seedling growth in particular will be harmed.

If you do not want to go to the trouble of making your own compost, JI composts can be bought ready mixed. The draw-back of these is that the loam will vary slightly from sample to sample, but not enough to affect the general properties of the composts.

SOILLESS AND SPECIALIZED COMPOSTS

Good loam may carry diseases and it is becoming scarce and expensive. As a viable alternative to the JI composts, soilless composts have been formulated by the University of California. Some plants will not thrive in ordinary soil-based or soilless composts, and need specialized composts.

SOILLESS COMPOSTS

These composts are made up of peat and sand. The most common formula is a 50:50 mix, though a 75:25 one is also popular. Nutrients and chalk are added to them. The sand is much finer than for a JI compost and the peat is granulated sphagnum peat. Soilless composts are almost exclusively proprietary, and each brand has a different blend of nutrients, which last for varying lengths of time. However, it is possible for you to make up your own soilless composts by using a proprietary compound fertilizer, such as 1½ level tablespoons of Phostrogen to 2 gal (9 litres) of a mixture of peat and perlite, plus the same quantity of chalk. Using this recipe as a basis, you can make up other mixtures varying the proportions of fertilizer, chalk, peat and perlite, or substituting fine sand for the perlite.

SPECIALIZED COMPOSTS

Cacti are one of the few groups of plants that do better in a specialized compost. They need one which dries out quickly and thus has much more drainage than most plants require. Use 3 parts JI No 1 diluted with 1 part grit. Another good formula is equal parts of loam, peat and coarse sand with a little bonemeal added. These formulae serve as a starting-point from which to experiment.

Bulb fibre consists of a mixture of 6 parts peat, 2 parts oyster shell or perlite and 1 part crushed

1 part peat   1 part sand   Chalk   Nutrients

Above: *Soilless composts are made up of peat and sand in a 1:1 or 3:1 ratio, plus a little chalk and plant nutrients; perlite can be used instead of sand.*

charcoal. As it contains no nutrients, bulbs grown in this compost have to be discarded after flowering, unless liquid-fed from the time they flower until the leaves begin to die down. Even so, they may never be really strong. Bulbs which you want to grow again or plant in the garden must be grown in a good potting compost.

Cuttings will root quicker if you use a good draining compost. Pure sand, perlite or vermiculite is quite feasible, or a mixture of any of these with peat, e.g. 1 part peat to 3 parts sand. Nutrients are not essential, but do repot cuttings in this type of compost into ordinary growing compost as soon as they have rooted well. Rooting is quite possible in potting compost, and if struck individually, you can leave cuttings in the compost until their roots fill the pot and then pot on, saving time and money.

HYDROPONICS

Hydroponics is a method of growing plants in nutrient

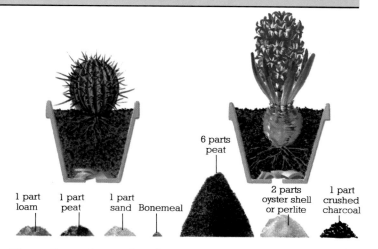

1 part loam   1 part peat   1 part sand   Bonemeal

6 parts peat

2 parts oyster shell or perlite   1 part crushed charcoal

Above: *For cacti, a good potting mixture can consist of equal parts by volume of loam, peat and sand, and a little bonemeal, to ensure vigorous root growth.*

Above: *Bulbs do well in this mixture, but will not flower again unless given weekly liquid feeding after flowering until the leaves die down.*

solutions alone, without any solid growing medium. The formulae for the various nutrient chemicals need careful calculations, and the question of salt build-up and the pH value both have to be constantly reviewed in order that the plants remain healthy.

THE pH SCALE

The pH scale of values indicates the degree of acidity or alkalinity of the soil moisture resulting

from the constituents of the soil or compost. The scale runs from 1 to 14, with 7·0 being the neutral point, and each number being 10 times the one preceding it. Up to 7 is acid; above it is alkaline, and the value can be found with test kits or meters which give a dial reading.

Below: *A soil kit gives the pH by comparing the soil solution colour with the test card, each colour representing a different pH value.*

NUTRIENTS AND FERTILIZERS

All living organisms need food to develop and reproduce. Plants obtain their food in two ways: by photosynthesis, and by absorption of particles of mineral nutrients through the root-hairs. A kind of two-way system operates in the plant's sap so that the minerals and chemicals combine in an enormous variety of permutations to fuel all its parts, including the leaves, flowers, fruits, seeds and stems. It is important that a plant has mineral nutrients, air and light in sufficient quantities, and in the correct ratio.

MINERAL DEFICIENCY DISORDERS

Photosynthesis is the process whereby water and carbon dioxide are absorbed in the presence of light to manufacture carbohydrates and oxygen. It can only take place in plants containing green colouring matter called chlorophyll. An essential part of chlorophyll is iron, and if a plant cannot absorb it, or it is actually lacking in the soil or compost, the green parts of the plant become yellow. Some plants are said to be calcifuges or lime-haters, because they are unable to absorb iron when it is contained in an alkaline soil. Such plants develop light yellow or cream-coloured leaves. This is a recognized common mineral deficiency disorder or disease, known as lime-induced chlorosis.

The research that went into the John Innes composts and the U.C. soilless mixtures took into account the plants' need for a balanced proportion of mineral nutrients and produced formulae which supplied them to a healthy level. Too high a concentration of a single element can damage a plant. The root hairs will lose moisture and ultimately the whole plant will become deprived of water; the effect is known as scorching.

Shortages of mineral nutrients can also have startling and

Right: *If plants lack a mineral element, they will show it by a variety of symptoms, such as leaf discolouration, poor flowering or stunting. Most important are nitrogen, phosphorus and potassium, plus trace elements.*

dramatic results. Deficiencies of major elements are particularly alarming, as plants require them most. The important three are nitrogen, phosphorus and potassium: all are absorbed in the form of compounds. In very general terms, nitrogen is involved in the production of leaves, stems and branches and phosphorus is essential to seedlings, young plants, roots and maturation. Potassium is associated with water balance, and flower, fruit and seed formation and it is used by commercial tomato growers as a booster when light is poor.

TRACE ELEMENTS

Minor minerals, such as magnesium, calcium and sulphur, are still comparatively important. 'Trace' elements—manganese, magnesium, boron, molybdenum and others—although essential, are only needed in very small quantities. Most loams contain sufficient trace and minor elements, but the major elements usually have to be incorporated, hence the base fertilizer in the JI composts and the addition of nutrients to the soilless mixtures.

NUTRIENT ANALYSIS

The analysis of nutrient content should be shown on fertilizer packs. It is also usually given for composts, generally as a ratio of percentages of the big three, thus: 7%N:7%P:7%K, being nitrogen, phosphorus and potassium respectively. Some composts contain sufficient plant food for the entire growing season, while others need boosting (see pp. 44-45).

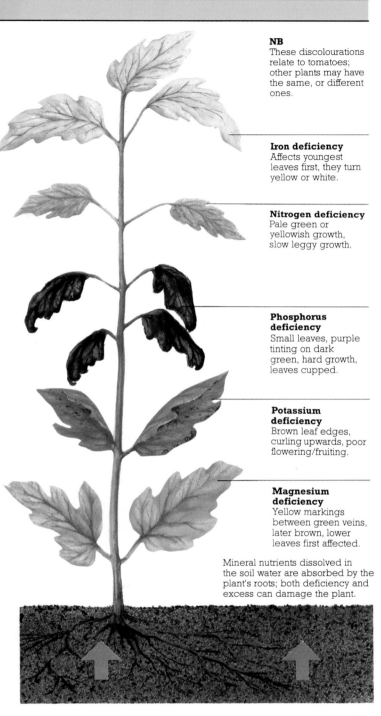

NB
These discolourations relate to tomatoes; other plants may have the same, or different ones.

Iron deficiency
Affects youngest leaves first, they turn yellow or white.

Nitrogen deficiency
Pale green or yellowish growth, slow leggy growth.

Phosphorus deficiency
Small leaves, purple tinting on dark green, hard growth, leaves cupped.

Potassium deficiency
Brown leaf edges, curling upwards, poor flowering/fruiting.

Magnesium deficiency
Yellow markings between green veins, later brown, lower leaves first affected.

Mineral nutrients dissolved in the soil water are absorbed by the plant's roots; both deficiency and excess can damage the plant.

POTTING

There are right and wrong ways of putting a plant into a pot or removing it, just as there are for any other gardening technique. In this case it can make all the difference between success and failure, between a happy, healthy, thriving plant and a sad and sickly, stunted one that may die.

WHEN TO REPOT

In general, plants already established in pots and other containers will outgrow their space and use up the nutrient in the course of one growing season. If you are constantly having to water a plant to prevent it wilting or dropping its flowers, or if its leaves and stems are turning yellow, it is a sure sign that it needs more room or fresh compost.

You can pot-on or repot at times other than spring. It depends on the state of the plant. With fast-growing plants, roots may fill the pot and even protrude from the drainage holes. This may occur as soon as halfway through the growing season. If this happens you may wish to pot-on. On the other hand, a 'pot-bound' plant often flowers better, and their constricted roots can help to contain the size of top growth: a method used in bonsai work.

Do not pot plants towards the end of their growing season, or 'overpotting' can occur. This is when the plant does not make use of the extra moisture available in the larger pot, because it has ceased to grow for the year. It then suffers, as the moisture becomes sour with the accumulation of waste products given off by the roots.

Remember that some plants, especially succulents from South Africa, have reversed seasons, so that any potting for them is done at the beginning of the British autumn.

POTTING-ON

When potting-on, make sure that the root-ball is moist all the

Plants need repotting about once a year, in spring; this primula is pot-bound, with its roots emerging from the drainage hole; turning the pot upside-

down onto one hand, knock it against the work surface, keeping a firm hold of it in the other hand, when the plant will fall safely out complete.

way through. Work on a perfectly clean, flat surface, and prepare the new, clean container.

Submerge new clay pots in water for about 24 hours. If you do not, they will constantly draw water out of the compost, away from the plant.

Turn the plant out. Remove any drainage material from its base. Then position it in the new pot so that the root-ball is about 1in-2in (25mm-50mm) below the rim. Large plants may need positioning deeper. Then fill the pot with compost. Hold the stem steady and upright with one hand and press the compost down with the fingers of the other, firmly for soil-containing com-posts, lightly for the soilless kind. Ram down the new compost for large plants firmly with a stick. For all plants new compost should be compacted to the same degree as the old, to ensure that water drains through at the same rate.

Tap the pot on the work surface once or twice to settle the compost and level it. Then water and allow the surplus moisture to drain out. Put it in a shaded, warm place for a day or two while it recovers. Water only lightly during this period, if at all; a newly-potted plant is almost a hospital case, and should be treated accordingly for a few days after the operation.

REPOTTING

Repotting is not carried out very often, and usually only with the larger, permanent plants, such as orange trees, camellias, and Swiss cheese plants. It is necessary to unwind and cut back some of the longer roots to the root-ball surface, and remove some of the compost, but make sure you cause as little injury to the remaining roots as possible. A good alternative is to topdress only by carefully removing the top 1in-3in (25mm-75mm) of compost, and replacing it with fresh compost, then maintaining the nutrient level with regular feeding applications during the plant's growing season.

Put drainage crocks, if needed, in the base of the pot, then a little compost. Use a pot about 2 sizes larger, and centre the plant in it so that the root-ball *surface is 1-2in (2-5cm) below the rim, and fill in compost round it; firm with the fingers, tap the pot gently on the bench to settle the compost, and water well.*

Greenhouse Management

In temperate climates plants start to grow new leaves and stems in spring, flower in summer, and set seed and fruit in autumn, thereafter dying completely, or becoming dormant in winter.

SEASONAL TEMPERATURE CHANGES

Growth is set off by rises in temperature and increases in light. Plants in glasshouses have to adapt themselves to much greater changes in temperature than they would outdoors. In summer, high temperatures generally remain steady, but in spring they can fluctuate enormously. Autumn temperatures gradually drop during the daytime throughout the season. There is often an early sharp frost in the first half of autumn, and periods of several nights, and days also in some years, of hard frost in late autumn. All of them come suddenly and can take even the weather forecasters by surprise.

CONTROLLING TEMPERATURE

Temperature control under cover must be aimed at cushioning the plants from extremes and maintaining steady warmth in the growing season, as well as giving protection from frost in the cool houses. Remember to keep a watchful eye on cold-house plants when frost is hard and prolonged.

In springtime, artificial heating in the cool-house is generally unnecessary during the day, unless the weather is unseasonable, but after dark some is likely to be necessary. In fact during the day the problem will be to keep the warmth from

scorching seedlings, small plants and cuttings rooted the previous summer. A temperature of 60°F-70°F (16°C-21°C) should be maintained at this time of year. Temperatures can be controlled by shading (see page 39), and by the manipulation of glasshouse ventilators and conservatory windows.

VENTILATION

Where you have a choice, open the ventilators on the side facing away from the prevailing wind. During the summer, you will probably need to leave ventilators wide open all day, and also the door(s), as most plants under cover do not appreciate temperatures higher than about 85°F (30°C). In autumn you will gradually open the ventilators less, and in winter you will rarely open them more than a crack. It is important to leave them open a little, however low the outside temperature, so that there is an exchange of air with the outside. It also helps to get rid of excess humidity resulting from condensation on the inside of the glazing.

ATMOSPHERIC HUMIDITY

Another important aspect of temperature control is the atmospheric humidity. In dry air and high temperatures, plants transpire much more vapour than they do in moist air. Their roots therefore absorb more water from the compost or soil than

Above: *Automatic ventilators will close of their own accord in cool conditions, as are likely to occur when it is raining.*

Below: *Humid air is vital to plant health, and those plants that need it most can be misted with water several times a day.*

usual. In high temperatures water evaporates quicker. One way of reducing the temperature is to increase the humidity by 'damping down'. This involves spraying the paths, staging, and plants with water during the hottest parts of the day. At the same time, this will decrease the rapid transpiration rate of the plants. In conservatories, misting the plants frequently is a great help on the hottest days.

Humidity combined with low temperatures encourages the spread of fungal disease, especially grey mould (*Botrytis cinerea*). Humidity in high temperatures results in bacterial disease problems. Dry atmospheres are always harmful to healthy plants except to cacti, pelargoniums and a few others. They can lead to infestations of red spider mite and scale insect.

To sum up, the aim is to combine warmth with freshness. If you feel comfortable in your greenhouse, the chances are your plants will too.

LIGHT AND SHADING

Management of greenhouse lighting does not require a great deal of work or time. Plant development is an exceedingly complex process, and many factors are involved, but broadly speaking it can be said that the more light a plant receives, the faster it will photosynthesize and the quicker it will grow. The glasshouse provides an increase in the temperature, but unavoidably cuts down on some of the available light.

TYPES OF GLAZING

The first glasshouses had green-tinted glass, containing air-bubbles. The panes were small, and the wooden glazing bars blocked out a good deal of light. Nowadays horticultural glass is smooth, transparent and unblemished, and it allows 90% transmission. It is usually fixed into a metal framework, mainly made of aluminium alloy. The use of this light and strong material permits a much narrower framework than the wooden bars.

Glass has its drawbacks, even so; it cracks and breaks easily and it is comparatively heavy. This is a consideration where you are growing crop plants and attaching them to the framework for support. Six tomato plants in full fruit with eight trusses set and swelling can weigh nearly a hundredweight. The synthetic glazing now available is much lighter in weight.

The best synthetic glazing is probably the rigid plastic polycarbonate, which is shatter- and bullet-proof. It allows 85% light transmission, which is exceptionally good for a plastic. There is also glazing made from acrylic, with a light trans-mission comparable to glass. It is ⅛in (2mm) thick, and can be sawn or drilled. It has a long life before it eventually becomes discoloured, it retains heat well, and is eight times stronger than glass. The plastic sheeting

Above: *There are various methods of shading greenhouses from summer sun, such as these outer wooden slatted blinds.*

used for walk-in tunnels and small houses cuts down light considerably, but the crop plants for which they are mainly used do not appear to suffer appreci-ably and in fact benefit from the shading provided in summer.

If plants are induced to grow in bad light by high temperatures and extra feeding, they will

Below left: *Blinds made of a synthetic linen-type of cloth can be fixed just under the roof or on the outside.*

Above: *Shading can be applied directly to the glass on the outside by painting on a proprietary rainproof mixture.*

become leggy, soft and vulnerable. On dull summer days, therefore, the temperature should be reduced, and during long periods of dull weather in summer, extra potash should be supplied. In winter, keep glazing as clean as possible so that whatever growth might occur is encouraged by the maximum light available.

ARTIFICIAL LIGHT

Artificial lighting can be used in winter to supplement the short, dull days, either by increasing the number of daylight hours or by intensifying the quality of the light. It is by manipulation of the light in this way that chrysanthemums are produced all year round by commercial growers. For the gardener, 200-watt mercury vapour lamps with tungsten filaments are the most practical sources of artificial light that are obtainable.

Plants that require plenty of light are generally hot-country plants, for example the pelargoniums from South Africa, the cacti from the Mexican deserts, and the bird of paradise flower, *Strelitzia reginae,* from the Cape of Good Hope. But many plants are not adapted to intense light, and the majority of tender and not-so-tender plants will not only grow well under glass but will actually need to have their leaves shaded from summer light.

SHADING

Shade can be provided in various ways. You can paint white or green shading on to the outside. There is one such brand which becomes translucent with rain. Alternatively there are roller blinds of wood laths, which fix on to the outside. Polypropylene netting, polythene sheeting or muslin are all suitable shading materials, and Venetian blinds look good in conservatories.

Plant Care

The question of watering causes more controversy and difficulties than any other aspect of container-growing, especially when the plants are in a completely artificial environment. Fortunately the drainage holes in the base of containers and the careful formulation of composts ensure that effective drainage occurs and allows aeration of the growing medium.

THE IMPORTANCE OF WATER

Water constitutes a large part of a plant's system. It is also the medium in which nutrients are carried, and absorbed into the roots. If plants have to do without it permanently they die: seedlings die within a few days. A plant needs water constantly present in the compost, but not so much that there is no air, as the roots cannot function without oxygen. Fortunately, there is some leeway between too much and too little. Clay pots help to act as buffers, and soilless composts are composed of ingredients which remain stable under widely-fluctuating water conditions.

WHEN TO WATER

The decision about when to water can be most easily deter-mined by asking yourself these five questions:
1 Is the compost a lighter brown than usual?
2 Does the surface feel dry?
3 Does the plant show signs of distress by wilting at midday when the temperature is highest, and has it been dropping its flowers soon after opening?
4 Does the container feel light-weight when lifted?
5 Does tapping the pot with a wooden stick produce a high-pitched sound rather than a dull, low thump?
If the answer is yes to any of these questions, water is necessary.

HOW MUCH WATER?

The amount to apply at each watering should be sufficient to fill the space at the top of the pot between the compost surface and the pot rim, when poured on fairly rapidly. In a well-structured compost this will percolate right through to the base, and any that is not absorbed on the way will drain out through the base holes. Provided the plant is being correctly watered, and has been potted in the right-sized pot, this is all that need be given at any one time.

If the plant has not been watered frequently enough, or if the central root-ball is more compressed than the compost on the outside one dose of water like this will not be enough, and a second should be given, pouring the water on slowly. If the plant has dried out so badly that the compost has caked and is shrivelling away from the pot sides, it will be necessary to moisten the centre by taking the plant in its container and submerging the pot in a bucket of water until

1

2

Above: *Water will not be absorbed with a badly dried out plant (**1**): plunge the pot into water (**2**) until bubbles stop appearing.*
Below: *Established plant being watered using a spout.*
Bottom: *Seedlings being sprayed with water using a rose.*

air-bubbles cease to rise to the surface. Allow the pot to drain for a few minutes after this before returning it to its home.

WATERING METHODS

A watering-can is the most convenient method of watering most container plants, preferably one made of galvanised metal with a long spout. This design is well-balanced and easy to handle, and the long spout allows you to reach plants at the back of the staging. The spray attachment, called a 'rose', can be obtained with different hole sizes. The small ones give a fine spray for seedlings, while the larger ones are for mature plants. The cans themselves come in different sizes, up to about 2 gal (9 litres). Plastic cans seem to attract algal growth on the inside, especially if water is left standing in them.

SUITABLE TYPES OF WATER

It is generally best to use water which is at atmospheric temperature. Some plants do better with warm water, such as the achimenes, whose common name is the 'hot-water plant'. It is also preferable to use either rainwater, which has been standing a day or two, or boiled water. Most plants do not like hard water.

41

SPECIALIZED WATERING

The quantity of water to give a plant depends on a great many factors. The golden rule is always fills the space at the top of a pot or container. If you give less, the base compost never gets any water, and the roots are encouraged to come to the surface, where they suffer even more as a result.

VARIATIONS ON THE RULE

Variations upon this rule depend on the type and size of plant, its stage of growth, its compost, and the temperature around it. Although it is exasperating to be advised, when you are inexperienced, that the plant will tell you when it needs water, this is in fact true. The signs are small, and this is where experience counts. An acutely-observant eye is developed by frequent examination of your own plants and those in display gardens and glasshouses, where they are grown to perfection. The latter will provide a good criterion for comparison when deciding if to water.

WATERING AND PLANT SIZE

The following guide suggests quantities of water to give:
Small: water approximately every third day, after drying has gone below the compost surface
Average: water whenever compost surface becomes dry
Large: water frequently, while compost is still moist: this may mean twice a day or giving twice as much at any one time. Here is a more specific guide to help you:

Water seedlings often, with a fine spray; young and mature plants quite often; mature plants with flowers or fruit, fast-growing, at high temperatures, or with thin leaves, often; cacti (spring/autumn), quite often; cacti (winter), bulbs, corms and tubers, only very occasionally.

Plants do not require nearly so much water when they are dormant, and at such times you should give them sufficient water to keep the compost just moist, so that the roots do not wither. Some plants must,

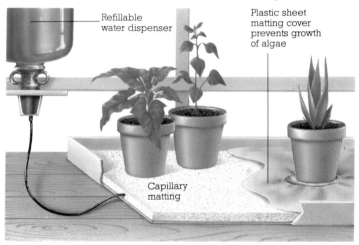

Refillable water dispenser

Plastic sheet matting cover prevents growth of algae

Capillary matting

Capillary watering: In which water is being constantly fed to plants via a wick in the pot drainage hole in contact with absorbent synthetic matting; in turn, this is supplied with water from the water dispenser above, which is filled by hand.

however, be kept dry. Often the bulbs, corms and tubers, and some of the cacti, can be allowed to become dry. In low temperatures, plants survive much better if the compost is almost dry; cold combined with wet when they are resting is practically always a death warrant.

IRRIGATION EQUIPMENT

Besides watering-cans, there is more sophisticated irrigation equipment available. For the larger greenhouse a hose with a variable spray attachment may be necessary. It is always better to apply soft water which is at atmospheric temperature, such as that standing in a tank or rain-water.

Capillary matting is a great boon if the plants have to be left all day, or time is short. The mat is kept moist from a tank acting as a reservoir. If you stand the plants on the mat the compost absorbs the water through the base of the pot by capillarity. Look for matting which has been treated to prevent the growth of algae, or buy an algicide. Alternatively you can use sand, in which case wicks must be inserted into the base of each pot to act as a channel for the water from the sand. Both matting and sand must be contained in trays on the staging.

Small-bore, flexible plastic pipes, called spaghetti piping, will provide trickle irrigation, in which water constantly drips through nozzles at the end of the pipes into individual pots. The pipes are attached to a sleeve on the main pipe, which in turn is connected to a reservoir. The quantity and frequency of water flow can be controlled by the nozzles, and by a screw within the tank.

Both these methods are extremely useful when the plants have to be left during holidays. The amount of water required by a given number of plants for a given period of time can be calculated. Provided the size of tank and the mains pressure are sufficient, your plants can be adequately watered in your absence without fail.

Water cistern

Leads to pots

Water supply to bench

Spaghetti tubing: *Each plant has one narrow tube fed by a large main one which derives its water supply from a cistern* *with a ballcock. Water drips steadily onto the compost and is especially good for plants during hot weather.*

43

PLANT FEEDING

The energy needed by plants to grow and develop is supplied by mineral particles as well as by carbohydrates formed during photosynthesis. Minerals are present in all soils, and are deliberately included in composts.

MINERALS IN COMPOSTS

The amount contained in JI No 1 is sufficient for plants grown in pots up to 3½in (9cm) in diameter. When the roots of these plants fill the pot, they will have exhausted the nutrient content and, on two counts, will be ready for a larger pot. JI No 2 is suitable for plants in pots up to 6in (15cm) diameter, and No 3 for pots up to 9in (23cm).

However, plants often stay permanently through the growing season in 4in (10cm) diameter pots and, although they do not grow too large for the pot, they do exhaust the nutrients in it, so you should give them extra food, usually from about halfway through the growing season. Plants which grow very quickly may need food faster than the average compost is able to yield it. For these, liquid or foliar

feeding (see below) is necessary. Small plants which grow slowly are happy all season. Cacti do not need extra food, though, contrary to general belief, they do require a potting compost which contains nutrients, like more conventional container-grown plants.

FERTILIZERS

Nutrients are supplied to container plants in several ways. Most fertilizers for this purpose are compounds, made up of the 'big three': nitrogen, phosphorus and potassium. Some of them contain other minerals such as iron, manganese and magnesium in a special form for lime-hating plants. The contents are always shown on the container.

Many of these compound fertilizers are supplied as powders, sometimes for dry application and sometimes for dissolving in water. Sprinkle dry powders evenly all over the surface of the compost, in the

Below: *Plants can be fed by using a dry powdery fertilizer, carefully measured out exactly, and sprinkled evenly all over the compost surface and watered in.*

quantity recommended by the manufacturer. A concentration in any one spot could damage the roots (see p. 32). Then water in the fertilizer at once. Never apply dry powders to dry compost, nor to plants which are in bad health. Similarly, only

Above: *Plants can also be fed by fertilizer spikes, which are pushed into the compost, or* (**below**) *by tablets of nutrient, which are also inserted.*

water powder fertilizers in solution on to moist compost.

Liquid fertilizers contain the same blend of minerals as dry ones. The solutions are usually concentrated and have to be diluted with water before use. Frequency of application is much greater than with powder formulations. On average once a week is enough, but like watering, this can vary depending on the type of plant, its growth rate, the compost and flowering or fruiting. Fast-growing plants, large plants and heavily-cropping plants will generally need liquid feed more than once a week.

Foliar feeding is a method used when you want instant results. It is usually a first-aid measure, for plants in dire need of nutrient. The plant absorbs the nutrients through the leaves directly into the cells where they may be needed most, rather than through the roots, and then conveyed to the top growth. However, this method is not used often in container-cultivation.

Some manufacturers have developed fertilizers in solid form, for convenience. These take the form of either plant sticks, tablets, or pellets, which dissolve slowly in the compost with watering. All you need do is apply one or more to each plant as recommended.

A slow-release fertilizer, in which the nutrients move slowly into the compost during many weeks, is generally incorporated into proprietary mixes. A controlled-release fertilizer is one which only releases the nutrients when the compost temperatures rise above a certain level, usually the one at which the plant starts to grow. Both these kinds of fertilizer are available separately and can be added to your own compost mixtures.

One of the most recently developed fertilizers contains the bacteria which convert nitrogen into the nitrates that plants can absorb through their roots.

If vegetation which has no useful function is allowed to remain on the plant, it will provide a centre for fungal diseases and shelter for insects including pests.

To maintain the plant in good health and to keep it looking immaculate, it is important to 'groom' it regularly. 'Grooming' usually needs to be done once a week; it is not a difficult job and it is particularly necessary in the conservatory where plants are so much on display.

Grooming is the removal of dead leaves and flowers and sometimes seeds or fruits, as of fuchsias, which will readily set fruit. Dead flowers left on plants inhibit the production of further flowers, because the plant is busy setting seed, and has no need to exert itself further in order to reproduce.

Stems and branches which are half-broken should be cut back cleanly, so should any with tips that shows signs of browning.

Leaf tips may also brown. If this is only slight you can allow them to remain, but if it is spreading into the whole leaf, it is preferable to remove it. Leaves resting on the compost surface can be a focus for discolouration and infection as well, so remove them when you see them.

As plants increase in size they must be regularly re-spaced. Move containers and pots further apart throughout the season to allow the plants extra space. You may find, even so, that some of them must be cut back.

PINCHING BACK

Training plants by pruning and pinching back is also part of the grooming process. To pinch back, nip out the tips of new shoots when they have about three pairs or sets of leaves. Late spring or early summer is the best time to do this. The object is to encourage the production of sideshoots which will carry flowers, so making the plant more attractive. It will delay flowering a little, but it is certainly worth remembering if you are planning to put any plants into a show or competition. Fuchsias benefit enormously from this practice, so do coleus (the flame nettle) and pelargoniums (geraniums).

PRUNING

Pruning is required for some of the shrubs. Again, fuchsias are very amenable to training into a variety of shapes, such as a standard, pyramid, pillar or espalier. Climbers also need pruning, more in the form of

Above left: *Many plants need support, even if they are not climbers. Split wire rings will attach stems of carnations or sweetpeas to stakes or canes, and are easy to use.*
Left: *An alternative is to use soft garden twine (fillis) for a neat tie that is not obvious.*

cutting-back to keep them within the space available, but it does also control the size of the root system: less top growth needs fewer roots to support it.

Pruning is mostly done at the start of the growing season, before repotting, and preferably just as the plants start to grow. Some further checking is necessary for some plants halfway through the season, in early summer.

SUPPORTS AND ATTACHMENTS

Many plants will need supports to look their best and to prevent the weight of flowers from breaking the whole plant down: tuberous begonias, for instance, have large and heavy, many-petalled flowers, as much as 6in (15cm) in diameter.

Split bamboo canes, rigid wire stakes, metal hoops with legs and metal wire stakes with a kind of chin-rest for the flower stalk are all useful forms of support. Trellis work and wire frameworks can be attached to walls, and plastic-covered wire frames, like a miniature trellis, provide adequate support for individual climbing plants. Plants can be attached to supports by green fillis (soft gardening string), wire rings, plastic tags or plastic-covered wire.

Plants still need some care after they have flowered. Some species require feeding until the leaves die down, to ensure flowering the following year. Others may simply be allowed to dry off, and the watering decreased until none is given at all. In winter, bulbs, corms and tubers rest completely and can often be left completely dry but free from frost. Other plants just tick over, and barely need to be watered at low temperatures. Cacti will not be harmed if watered only once or twice in winter, and will even resist slight frost.

Increasing Plants

There is an art to growing plants successfully from seed sown in containers. It is not difficult to learn, but there are some apparently unimportant points which can make all the difference between good and bad germination.

GERMINATION REQUIREMENTS

Seeds must have certain conditions in which to germinate. Moisture, and in most cases darkness, are essential, and nutrients are required for the emerging roots, although some are contained in the seed coat. Most plants germinate well at 60°F to 70°F (16°C to 21°C). Sub-tropical plants prefer a temperature between 70°F and 80°F (21°C and 27°C).

Containers must be spotlessly clean, whether they are clay pans, plastic half-trays, full-sized wooden seed boxes or 2in (5cm) pots. All should have holes in the base for drainage. Clay containers must already be thoroughly moist. Use composts specifically for seed-sowing because their properties permit adequate drainage and aeration, and because they contain higher proportions of phosphorus, which are needed by the roots of seedlings as they germinate.

HOW TO SOW SEEDS

If you are using soilless compost, you can put it straight into the container without using drainage materials on the base. Make sure it is moist, and fill the container to the rim. Firm down lightly with the fingers, first at the sides and in the corners and then in the centre. Add more if necessary to ensure that the final level is about ½in (15mm) below the rim, then tap the container lightly on the work-top

The compost for seed sowing should be evenly firm throughout and have a level surface; a wooden block will ensure this.

Seed must be sown all over the compost, and one method of sowing seed evenly is to place it in the palm and gently tap it out.

to settle the compost evenly.

Soil-containing seed compost should also be moist. Place pieces of broken clay pot over the drainage holes. Fill the containers with compost to the top, and compress it firmly. The surface can be levelled with a special tool. If the composts are not evenly firm, the seedlings will germinate at different depths.

Water soil-containing compost by putting the container into a shallow tray of water and leaving it to soak until the surface is dark and obviously moist. If necessary water soilless compost in the same way. It should only take a few minutes. Do not allow the compost to become waterlogged and soggy.

Warm compost will encourage germination, and for this heated propagators are helpful. Sow the seeds thinly and evenly all over the compost surface. If you are using individual containers, sow two or three seeds in each one. Then cover with a fine layer of compost, preferably put through a household sieve. Some seeds are so tiny as to be almost invisible, e.g. begonia seeds. These should be mixed with fine sand to help distribution and to show where they have been scattered. They need not be covered with compost.

Most seeds germinate in the dark, so either cover them in the traditional way, with brown paper on top of a pane of glass, or in the modern way, with a black plastic sheet. In the latter case condensation must be wiped off daily. Some seeds will only germinate in light, and this information will be noted on the seed packet when it is known. Unfortunately there are varieties for which light requirements are unknown.

STRATIFICATION

Stratification is a special method of encouraging seed germination. Dormancy in some species is difficult to break because the seeds have an exceptionally tough coat. Such seeds can be placed in layers (stratified) in sand, protected with a fine-mesh wire grid from mice, and left outdoors for the winter. This technique is mostly applied to hardy seeds.

LABELLING

Label seeds as soon as they are sown. It is amazing how easy it is to forget what you have sown, particularly when there are several varieties in one container. Record the date, too.

Once the seeds are sown, those of most plants should be given a fine covering of compost, sieved on with a very fine sieve.

The final stage is to label the tray with the name and date of sowing, doing this at the time with an indelible pencil.

SEEDLINGS: CARE AND TREATMENT

Once the seeds have begun to germinate, the cover should be taken off immediately, even if the seedlings are not all through. If the cover remains on, those that are growing will quickly become spindly. This will give them a poor start and they will never make good plants. Place them where the light is good, but not in hot sunlight, as they will easily scorch and the compost surface will dry rapidly. If they were sown thickly, thin them a little, removing weaklings and the late starters.

Keep the compost moist. At first this may simply mean watering lightly with a fine spray, but as they grow, more thorough watering becomes necessary, though still with a fine spray. Keep them warm, particularly at night. In most cases, the same temperature as was recommended for germination is suitable for seedling growth.

Seedlings that have grown from broadcast—that is, sown all over the surface of a container—must be pricked out when large enough. If left in the seed

Above: *If seeds have been sown in trays, the seedlings should be moved when large enough to handle. Dig them carefully out of the compost with*

a widger and hold them by one seed leaf. Make a hole in the new compost and, again using the widger, lower the seedling into the hole.

Above: *The leaves should rest on the compost. Fill the hole with compost, breaking the roots as little as possible. Most important, try to preserve*

the rounded tips, as it is through these that a seedling absorbs most of the phosphorus it will ever need as a mature plant. The roots should be spread out.

compost, they will run out of food and become leggy. Their roots will tangle, and growth will be altogether unsatisfactory, as they fight for space, air, water and nutrient.

PRICKING OUT

If the seeds are large enough to have been sown in potting compost in individual pots, they can be left alone, apart from watering, until their roots fill the pot, and then they should be potted on. If they have been sown two or three to a container, they should be thinned to leave only one seedling, the strongest and fastest-growing. If the seed is in seed compost, prick it out when it starts to produce its first true leaf.

You can prick out into individual 2in (5cm) pots of potting compost, or into trays of compost like the seed trays, prepared in the same way. In individual pots the seedlings can be left for longer before potting. In trays, the roots have more room to expand, though this may lead to problems when it comes to removing them for potting.

Seedlings are ready to prick out when they develop their seed leaves, and the first true

Above: A box of pricked-out seedlings, about 2in (5cm) apart each way, with the stems buried; planted this deep, the seedlings grow strong stems.

leaf has just appeared. Usually a pair of very simple small, oval or pointed leaves at the end of the stem constitute the seed leaves. Do not delay pricking out until after the full development of the second true leaf. Choose seedlings which are obviously healthy, and about the same size, so that they develop at the same rate. Discard any that are damaged and those with uneven seed leaves, unless this is a characteristic of the plant.

Dig the seedling carefully out of the compost with a widger, lifting it with its roots as intact as possible. It is particularly important to make sure that the root tips are not broken off. Any that are will have a square end to the root, instead of a rounded tip. It is at the tips of the roots and root-hairs that practically all the moisture and nutrients are absorbed, and seedlings that have lost these tips take much longer to establish, and will wilt quickly. While levering the seedling out, hold it gently by a leaf so that it does not become bruised.

Prepare a hole of a sufficient depth and width in the compost to receive the seedlings. Lower it into the hole with its roots spread out, until the stem is buried up to the seed leaves. This is to ensure that it has a strong stem when adult. A seedling which is left with an unsupported length of stem after pricking out becomes weak and is likely to flop over or break off as it grows. Firm the compost round it well.

With a tray or pan, it pays to make all the holes in advance, so that they are evenly spaced. They should be about 2in (5cm) apart from each other. The average tray can take 4 rows of 6 seedlings, or as many as 5 rows of 6, if they are very small.

After pricking out, water in the seedlings well, with a fine spray, and put them in a shady, warm place to recover.

SOFT STEM CUTTINGS

Seeds are the first things people think of in connection with increasing plants. Most of those that are available nowadays will produce plants exactly the same as each other and the parent plants, unless they are specifically sold as mixtures, but seeds collected at random from garden plants may produce quite different ones as regards flower colour, height, size or habit of growth. Varieties and hybrids are prone to this variation, species less so. If you want to grow new plants which will be exactly the same as their parents, you should increase them by vegetative methods, rather than the sexual ones involved with seed formation.

Above: *Pieces of stem can be made to produce roots; here a semi-mature stem is used to increase a geranium.*

Many plants which are grown under glass are increased by vegetative methods, such as stem cuttings, leaf cuttings, offsets, plantlets and air-layering. Geraniums and fuchsias are two of the plants regularly propagated by stem cuttings. This method, whereby pieces of a plant's stem are encouraged to produce roots from its base, is one of the most common. Some plants do this quickly and easily. Others need a good deal of help and are a great test of a gardener's expertise.

There are several different kinds of stem cuttings: the most familiar are called soft, or tip cuttings, semi-hardwood or half-ripe cuttings, and hardwood or ripe cuttings. The first two are the kinds which need the protection and warmth of glass. The hardwood kind are placed outdoors, and left there through the winter.

ENCOURAGING ROOTING

Plants have a natural tendency to produce roots from any tissue which has been injured. They do this most of all just below the junction of leaf and stem, which is called the leaf-joint, or node

to use the technical term (an internode is the piece of stem between two leaf-joints). If you cut off a stem just below the leaf-joint, it attempts to continue living by growing roots at the area of injury. By giving the stem the right conditions and refining the process of cutting, you can manipulate it to root and grow into a perfectly good new plant, exactly like the one from which it was taken.

WHEN TO TAKE
SOFT CUTTINGS

Stems to use for soft or tip cuttings are new ones, not yet a year old, which began growth in the spring. The time to take the cutting is between late spring and mid-summer, or whenever there are new shoots with tips that are still green and succulent.

HOW TO TAKE
SOFT CUTTINGS

Cut off the end of the shoot so that it is about 3in-3½in (7·5cm-9cm) long, approximately ½in (15mm) below the leaf joint. If it has a flower or flower bud on it, rooting may occur only with difficulty or not at all. Trim the

Above: *The cutting is trimmed cleanly, just below a leaf-joint, and the lowest leaf and leaf-stalk removed completely.*

Below: *The cutting is inserted in a hole made with a widger, at the side of a pot, to half its length, with the base firmly on the bottom.*

cut end neatly to immediately below the leaf-joint, and cut off the lower leaves cleanly, together with their stalks.

Put the cutting into moist cutting compost at the side of a pot, to a depth of about half its length. Rest the base of the cutting directly on the compost, and fill in round the cutting, firmly if you are using soil-containing compost, and lightly if you are using a peaty type. Three or four cuttings will fit in round the edge of a 3½in (9cm) pot. You can put one in the middle too.

Then cover the pots with a clear, blown-up, plastic bag.

Secure it with a rubber band and put the pots into a warm shady place. Check the cuttings every few days to make sure the compost is moist, and remove any fallen leaves which might be infected with grey mould.

It is extremely important to prevent any water loss from the leaves occurring, from the time the cutting is taken to when it is well rooted. It has no roots with which to replace the moisture, so it will wilt quickly. If the leaves stop carrying on photosynthesis, there will be no materials to set the root-making process in motion.

HALF-RIPE AND LEAF CUTTINGS

HALF-RIPE CUTTINGS

Half-ripe cuttings are taken later in the season, from early to late summer. The main difference is that the stem will have begun to harden and turn brown at the base, so that the cutting will only be soft and green at the very tip. Sometimes these cuttings have a heel; they can be torn off the stem so that a sliver of bark from the parent stem comes away with them, so that they are really sideshoots rather than tips. The heel helps in rooting, as it provides a larger area from which roots can grow.

Rootings of both these and soft cuttings may take a few days or up to a month. Treat half-ripe cuttings in the same way as soft stem cuttings. When the cutting starts to lengthen, remove the covering and spray or mist it until it is well established.

LEAF CUTTINGS

Roots can be produced by other parts of the plant's tissue, for instance the leaves, which can develop into plantlets. Some plants will do this without help: the plant sometimes called

Above: *Sweet bay can be increased by heel cuttings, short sideshoots torn off so that a sliver of bark and older tissues are attached.*

hen-and-chickens, *Tolmiea menziesii,* is an example. Plantlets are produced spontaneously on the surface of the leaf above the main vein, and they develop roots. When they are ready to establish themselves in the soil, they drop of their own accord, and so the plant spreads rapidly.

Leaf cuttings are made in summer, and plants which can be increased like this include *Begonia rex* varieties, the Iron Cross begonia, *B. masoniana,* and streptocarpus, gloxinia, African violets, sansevieria and succulents. They will all root most successfully at 65°F-70°F (18°C-21°C), especially if the compost itself is warm.

Cut off well-developed begonia leaves with a small piece of stem attached. Make small cuts through the main veins on the under-surface, near the junction with smaller veins. Lay the leaves on the surface of a cuttings compost, or a mixture of equal parts peat and coarse sand, with the stem helping to anchor them. The cut portions of the veins should touch the compost, and one or two small pebbles may be put on the leaf to ensure this, but not more. Then lightly water the leaves with a fine spray, and cover the container to keep the atmosphere round the leaf moist. Remove the covering daily to ventilate the leaf. In the close atmosphere this is necessary, as rotting can often occur.

In a few weeks small leaves will start to appear on the parent leaf surface, a sign that rooting has started. The subsequent plantlets can be detached when plenty of root is present, and potted into individual 2in (5cm) pots.

An alternative method is to use a piece of leaf about 1½in

(4cm) long, roughly three-sided, and containing a portion of one of the main veins. Push it upright into the compost at the side of the container to about a quarter of its length so that the unburied part will be supported by the side of the container when leaves appear at the base.

Streptocarpus are increased by cutting the leaf into sections crosswise, each about 2in (5cm) long, and burying them to a quarter of their length. Sansevieria are increased in the same way, though the new plants will not have the yellow edge that the parent did. This is one of the very few occasions when a plant reproduced vegetatively is not exactly like its parent, because this variety of sansevieria is a chimaera, a plant in which the outer layer of tissue cannot produce chlorophyll. The plantlets of sansevieria come from the inner, green part.

Succulent-leaved plants will also root readily from individual leaves, provided the compost has a sandy surface. Small ones can be laid flat and pressed lightly into the surface. Large ones should be allowed to dry for two days or so, and pushed in upright, cut end down.

To take African violet leaf cuttings simply push healthy mature leaves, complete with their stalks, into a moist soilless compost, around the edge of a pot. Each stem should be about 2in (5cm) long, cut cleanly straight across its base, and buried up to the leaf. They can also be encouraged to produce roots in water, though this takes rather longer, and it can be tricky to wean them from the water into compost.

Above left: *Sansevieria can be increased from leaf cuttings, cut crosswise into 2in (5cm) pieces.*

Left: *Inserted upright, they will produce plants with plain green leaves, not the variegated kind of the parent.*

INCREASING PLANTS: VARIOUS METHODS

Plants are way ahead of human beings in the number and diversity of ways in which they can ensure the continuance of their species. Stem and leaf cuttings can turn into new plants, exactly like their parents, and seeds may produce new varieties and types which are stronger and better able to survive than their predecessors. Here are four other methods whereby greenhouse plants can reproduce.

PLANTLETS

Some plants reproduce themselves in miniature as plantlets, actually growing on the plant. Such parents may not have many flowers, or they may grow where the means for pollination and fertilization are in short supply. A glasshouse plant which carries plantlets along the margin of its leaves is the succulent, *Bryophyllum daigremontianum.* The new plants are tiny, about ½in (15mm) tall, and will fall off when they reach this size and are ready to root. The spider plant, *Chlorophytum elatum* 'Variegatum', is another of this type, but its plantlets grow at the end of what would otherwise be flowering stems. They, too, grow roots in mid-air, and can be cut off and planted in individual pots. In its natural environment the stems would simply bend down until they were low enough for the roots to touch the soil.

The hen-and-chicken plant, *Tolmiea menziesii,* grows plantlets on the upper surface of its leaves and if they are not detached, they will fall and ensure their own survival.

OFFSETS

Most bulbs concentrate on reproducing by offsets, which are small bulbs, produced at the side of the parent or new-season bulb. Examples of these in the glasshouse include the sweetly scented freesias, the Cape cowslip, *Lachenalia tricolor,* and the hot-water plant, *Achimenes.*

Below: *The spider plant has plantlets at the end of each stem, which can be pegged into compost, when they should root.*

Above: *Division can sometimes be used: here a begonia tuber is cut into sections. Each must have buds, or they will not grow.*

They produce them in such numbers it is not worth keeping the small ones. The largest will be so plentiful that you are likely to have twice as many the following season. Bulbs, corms and tubers need feeding as the leaves die down, to ensure flowers the following year. They also need warmth to ripen, but not above 80°F (27°C), otherwise they may become 'sleepers', which means they will not develop at the right time, if at all. Some need to be kept completely dry, others require a little moisture while dormant.

Some plants in this group can actually be cut into sections. Begonia tubers which have become large, or cyclamen corms are good examples. Provided they are healthy and the cut surface is dusted with a fungicidal powder, and provided each piece has a growing point or two in the form of a dormant bud or 'eye', they will grow into normal plants. Such cutting should be done just as growth is beginning. There is one begonia, *B. sutherlandii*, which will grow bulbils from its leaf-joints with great freedom,

and these will drop off onto the soil to form miniature plants the following season.

DIVISION

Division is a method familiar to outdoor gardeners, as it is used for herbaceous perennials. If you are careful some glasshouse plants, such as African violets, Cape primroses *Streptocarpus* and the Italian bell flower *Campanula isophylla,* can be increased in this way as the growth season is beginning. Try not to injure the plants any more than can be helped, and use a sharp knife to cut through the crown. The places to make the divisions are usually obvious.

Keep the youngest parts of the plants, not the old centre, and remove the long roots, old roots and any which are brown and rotting. Take away any old stems and leaves, and replant with new compost into containers which will not cramp the roots. Plants which can be increased in this way will naturally divide themselves into new plants.

AIR LAYERING

For glasshouse gardeners who have been successful with stem cuttings, the method of increasing known as air-layering can be tried. The classic plant on which to try this is the rubber plant, *Ficus elastica,* and the principle is the usual one of injuring the plant, and then supplying the optimum conditions for root production. However, make the injury while the stem is still attached to the plant: a slanting, partial cut through the stem opposite a leaf joint, which you must then keep open with a match-stick. Remove the leaf and its stalk. Bind fibrous peat or sphagnum moss round the cut stem and secure the whole with clear polythene sheet to make a 'sausage'. With warmth, rooting will occur in 2-3 months.

PROPAGATORS

While it is perfectly possible to produce new plants without the use of artificial heat, it does help with the propagation of a much greater variety of ornamentals, and with the harvesting of vegetables and fruits at times when they are expensive to buy. Moreover, there is no doubt that propagating packs do streamline the work, and if you are growing pot plants from seed or cuttings in quantity for market stalls or garden fêtes, they do make life easier.

UNHEATED PROPAGATORS

There are propagating packs, which generally consist of a container with a number of small pots, a self-watering base and a transparent lid or domed cover. One well-known type is made of expanded polystyrene and has separate pot-like compartments to take seed or cuttings. Although sold without a lid, separate rigid, transparent covers made by other companies can be obtained and used to fit over this, or seed-trays.

Other unheated propagators may consist of small square peat pots joined together in batches of 40 or so, complete with a plastic tray into which they fit exactly, and a clear rigid plastic cover. There are also extra-large

Above: *A pop-up propagator's compressor board can be used in reverse for pushing out the plantlets and their root-balls.*

containers, 3in (7·5cm) deep, 22in (55cm) long and 10in (25cm) wide, with domed transparent covers 5½in (14cm) deep, in which are fitted adjustable ventilators. It is worth looking at a variety of types.

Unfortunately, these plastic covers tend to become opaque with time, so losing their original light transmission, but they do protect the young seedlings or rooted cuttings, and maintain atmospheric humidity.

HEATED PROPAGATORS

A more complex propagator is the heating panel, which is electric, and plugs into a mains point. These vary in size and therefore cost. The cheapest, with a wattage of 25, is a few pounds. The largest, with a wattage of 75, is about five times as much. Some of these can be bought as a starting point and the containers and covers added to them as time, money and space allow. Some will take one seed tray, others will take two or the equivalent in pots.

Then there are the most sophisticated propagators with the heating contained in a covered base. One of the most useful ones will accommodate four of the smaller trays, has built-in ventilation and two adjustable louvres in the top of the cover. There are many variations on this heating theme. Some have adjustable temperature control and/or thermostatic control.

'De luxe' heated propagators are almost miniature green-houses, and can be used as such for your more prized or delicate plants, after propagation has finished. One model has a glazed top with an aluminium frame, sliding doors, a wattage of 50, and a variable thermostat. The base is 30in x 16in (75cm x 40cm). Another, for the dedicated gardener, contains a misting unit, from which moisture is

Above: *Some propagators consist of a metal base plate, electrically heated, on which the pots or seed-trays are stood, covered with a clear plastic top.*

given off automatically at set intervals. It is contained in a circular propagator, with a ground area of roughly 1 sq yd (1 sq m). It comes complete with four wedge-shaped trays, designed to fit the circular base, and it stands approximately 17in (42cm) high.

Another method of providing basal warmth is by soil-heating cables which, as well as being placed in the soil of a glasshouse border, can be obtained in kits for inserting into propagating boxes. These are moisture proof, insulated and have a copper earth screen. Some are thermo-statically controlled.

It is very well worth investing in a heated propagator, even the smallest. If you can manage a two-tray one, or even one of the large models, to which the cover can be added later, you can use clear plastic sheeting on a wire framework in the meanwhile.

Even if you do not use the whole of the base for germinating seeds or striking cuttings, it can be used when the plantlets need individual pots or have to be pricked out, at a time when the natural temperature is too low in the conservatory or green-house. Raising plants is not difficult. It is bringing them to maturity when there are not the right temperatures which can be tricky. A heated propagator will widen your horizons enormously.

AVOIDING TROUBLE

In spite of the temptation to crowd everything possible into the propagators, try to avoid doing so. It encourages disease to spread, and plants can become leggy and pale. Even when it is important to maintain a humid atmosphere, you should keep a little air circulating in the propagator. Put the propagator in a good light, or sunlight, provided it has a cover, and make sure the compost is always moist. Wipe off any condensation on the cover daily.

Trouble-shooting

The confined environment of a greenhouse or conservatory, filled with healthy plants, growing in mostly warm temperatures, provides ideal conditions for insects and fungi to thrive. Insects and similar pests can be extremely difficult to dislodge completely once they have got a foothold. The first line of defence is to make absolutely certain that any plants obtained, by buying or as gifts, are completely free of such pests as red spider mite or whitefly.

Scale insects are easily missed on plants. They infect palms, stag's horn ferns and hippeastrums in particular. They manage to insinuate themselves between sheathing stems, and where new leaves are beginning to shoot, but if they are present, there will usually be one or two out in the open.

CLEANING YOUR GREENHOUSE

Where a greenhouse is clean and free from such problems, it can be kept in that condition with a regular clean. The end of the season, from early to mid-autumn, when many plants have finished their lives or are coming to the end of their growth for the year, is often a good time. If the winter that follows is cold and keeping plants alive is difficult, grey mould will be a major problem, and probably other diseases as well, so a clean out in early spring is also advisable.

For the autumn turn-out, empty the whole greenhouse or conservatory. If you put the plants outside while the weather is still warm, you can wash and scrub down the whole of the inside of the house, including the panes, the framework, the staging, the ventilators, and the concrete

paths. Wooden staging needs a particularly good clean as it provides an excellent roosting place for over-wintering insects. Use hot water and a soap washing-up liquid, household bleach or a sterilizing solution of a proprietary tar-oil-based household disinfectant. If pests have invaded the greenhouse, a solution of formalin, obtainable from chemists, diluted in the proportion of 1:50, i.e. 1 part formalin to 49 parts water can be used instead for washing and scrubbing. Although effective, it smells unpleasant, and is irritating to the eyes, nose and mouth. Wear a mask and rubber gloves while using it. Plants should not be returned to the house until the smell has completely gone.

All containers and all other equipment must be cleaned thoroughly. Either scrub watering-cans and sprayers free of green algae, or leave a solution of household bleach inside them overnight. Throw out rubbish which has accumulated, and sort out labels and other items where insect pests might hide.

Any plants returning to the greenhouse, such as chrysanthemums, evergreen plants, winter-flowering varieties, or young plants over-wintering for

next year's planting out, should be given a clean bill of health. Remove any kind of decaying unwanted vegetation, and check over their containers. If shading has been applied to the glazing, the autumn is the time to clean it off. Make sure the glazing is as clean as possible, ready for the dull short days of winter.

At the end of winter, another small clean will be necessary. It can be done at the same time as the annual repotting and pruning of the plants. Do not use formaldehyde this time, as the outside temperature will not be high enough to leave the plants standing outdoors. Soapy water is a good substitute.

Above: *To ensure maximum light, the green growths between overlapping panes should be scraped out, and washed down.*

Below: *The greenhouse should be thoroughly hosed down with a detergent solution, and then water, to remove dirt and grease.*

PLANT HEALTH AND HYGIENE

Good control of pests and diseases in a greenhouse is vital. If they are allowed to spread, ornamentals become unsightly and stunted, crop plants fail to yield, and some insects or fungi become ineradicable.

One of the most important points is to make sure that any plants which are obtained, whether from friends, a garden centre or a florist, are clean and free from this kind of trouble. It is all too easy to introduce a palm or stag's horn fern with scale insect infestation, or a primula with roots which are being eaten by vine weevil grubs, or to buy tomato plants infected with grey mould. Examine the plants carefully while buying and at home. If possible repot them at once. Many will need a larger pot and new compost in any case. Then any root-aphids, grubs, rotting roots, etc., will become apparent, and action can be taken before it is too late.

Secondly, keep everything free from dirt and debris at all times. Clean all pots, seedtrays and containers of every kind before use. Keep tools spotless, and wash out watering-cans and sprayers at regular intervals.

Once red spider mite has infested the inside of a greenhouse, complete eradication is extremely difficult. You may have to remove all the plants, sterilize the inside of the house, and perhaps even scrap the plants and start with new specimens. The glasshouse version of this mite breeds all year round, laying its eggs in inaccessible crevices in framework and staging. The minute size of the creatures and their eggs makes chemical control very difficult. Even biological control is not always totally satisfactory.

Thirdly, remember that unsuitable conditions for the plants will render them vulnerable to infestation on an epidemic scale. Too high a temperature, combined with a dry atmosphere, resulting in dry roots, will encourage a population explosion. A dry atmosphere, but with

Red spider mite infesting primula leaves, which are speckled pale yellow; mites will be found on the underside of the leaves.

Greenfly (aphids) can be effectively controlled without using insecticide by finger and thumb removal day by day.

root moisture, will induce mildew, and high humidity combined with a cool, dull environment will promote the rapid spread of grey mould and other diseases. If you maintain the right conditions, natural predators and parasites are likely to be present, though mostly unseen, and these can be a natural way of controlling pests. The aim is to ensure warmth, and a slightly moist, well-ventilated atmosphere, while providing enough water in the growing medium to keep the plants from wilting.

Keep a very watchful eye on the plants, particularly the undersides of leaves, where most pests feed and breed. A quick examination first thing every day pays enormous dividends in plant health, and if pests are present, manual control with finger and thumb as soon as they are seen will often be sufficient to check the outbreak completely. Similarly, daily removal of leaves, stems and flowers which are broken, discolouring, or obviously disease-infected, will stop an infection before it can kill.

If an outbreak has slipped through these defences, more stringent control measures will be needed. Red spider mite, whitefly and caterpillars can be treated biologically: that is, with the use of predators and parasites. These 'biological control' insects can be obtained in proprietary packs, together with instructions for use. Once the pest has been eliminated, the parasites and predators will also eventually die.

If chemical control becomes necessary, apply exactly according to the manufacturer's directions, and treat the under-side of leaves in particular. Most pesticides for home greenhouse use are formulated as sprays. Dusts have become much less popular. There are a few in smoke form, but they are unsuitable for conservatories. Soil drenches are occasionally necessary where root pests have been at work, and aerovaps, which release chemicals into the atmosphere, are available.

Mealy bug is a difficult pest to control, as it is protected with white waxy fluff; remove bodily and spray with an insecticide.

Scale insects encrust stems and leaves of many greenhouse plants, feeding on their sap. Once established, they stay put.

PESTS AND DISEASES

Symptoms on leaves	Cause
Puckered, curled, sometimes with yellowing; tiny green or black insects on undersides	Greenfly, blackfly
Dull grey-green or speckled yellow; silky webs; curling and withering; minute red, pink or white dots on undersides	Red spider mites
Grey-green, curled, sticky; sometimes black patches; tiny, white moth-like insects on undersides	Whitefly
Holes in leaves high up on plant	Caterpillars
Irregular holes in leaves low down	Snails, slugs
Small brown or pale green bumps on underside, near veins and on edges	Scale insects
Fluffy white blobs on upper and undersides	Mealy bugs
Winding pale green lines, or biscuit-coloured blisters on upper surfaces, leaves wither	Leaf-miners
Small silvery patches (also on flowers)	Thrips
Small, semi-circular holes in leaf edges	Adult vine weevils
Leaves sickly, grey-green (no plant growth)	Root aphids, larvae of vine weevils
Grey fur on upper/lower surfaces, leaves brown or yellow in these areas	Grey mould
Powdery white patches on upper surface, leaves curling	Powdery mildew
Black patches	Sooty mould, grows on honeydew
Sticky patches	Honeydew from aphids, scale insects, whitefly
Small, raised, red-brown spots on undersurfaces	Rusts
Distortion, curling, yellow mottling or blotching (plant stunted)	Viruses
Seedlings eaten at soil level roots of mature plants at drainage holes eaten clearly off	Woodlice (Pill bugs)
Plants wilt suddenly and collapse; stem at soil level (collar) soft and rotting	Basal stem rot or bacterial rot of melons
Plants do not grow; leaves small, poor colour, misshapen roots with bumps	Root-knot eelworm

Remedy	Pesticide chemicals
Permethrin, pyrethrum, malathion, pirimicarb	*Benomyl* systemic, protectant, eradicant fungicide, non-toxic, except to earthworms
Malathion, dimethoate, rotenone, *Phytoseiulus similis* (predator)	*Derris, see Rotenone*
Permethrin, *Encarsia formosa* (parasite)	*Dimethoate* insecticide, organophosphorus, systemic through leaves, toxic to fish, birds and some plants, see directions for use
Hand-pick; permethrin, rotenone, HCH (BHC)	*HCH (BHC)* insecticide, organochlorine, toxic to bees, fish, animals and some plants, moderately persistent
Methiocarb, metaldehyde	
Malathion, dimethoate	*Malathion* insecticide, organophosphorus, non-persistent, toxic to fish, birds, bees and some plants
Malathion, dimethoate under pressure	
Hand-pick; dimethoate	*Permethrin* insecticide, synthetic pyrethroid, lasts 3 weeks, safe on plants, virtually no effect on mammals
Pyrethrum, permethrin	*Metaldehyde* molluscicide, anaesthetic effect, toxic to birds, fish and mammals
HCH (BHC)	
Wash compost off roots; remove maggots or white patches; re-pot in fresh compost; water with malathion	*Methiocarb* molluscicide, carbamate, toxic to fish, birds and mammals
Hand-pick; benomyl, tecnazene	*Piperonyl butoxide* chemical which increases the effectiveness of pyrethrum without toxic effects
Hand-pick; benomyl, propiconazole	*Pirimicarb* insecticide, carbamate, specific to aphids (greenfly, blackfly), moderately persistent, not plant toxic
Sponge off	
Sponge off, control insects	*Propiconazole* fungicide, systemic, a protectant and eradicant, toxic to fish
Hand-pick; spray with propiconazole	*Pyrethrum* insecticide, plant origin, non-persistent, non-toxic
Destroy affected plants	
Boiling water, HCH (BHC) dust	*Rotenone (derris)* insecticide, plant origin, non-persistent, toxic to bees and fish
Destroy affected plants, including roots; do not replant in same soil	
Destroy plant completely; discard compost; sterilize containers and equipment	*Tecnazene* fungicide, non-systemic, longlasting, low toxicity

Frames

Frames are sometimes regarded as a cheap alternative to a full-size greenhouse, or as a substitute for one if space is limited. They are quite adequate for raising crop plants, such as melons, tomatoes, lettuce, strawberries or sweet peppers, which remain in the frame for their entire life-cycle, but they are not really suitable for display, nor will they accommodate tall plants.

TYPES OF FRAME

Like glasshouses, frames can be of timber or metal with glass or synthetic glazing. They can be span-roofed (double-span), or single-span, and there are many different variations, within a wide price range.

USES FOR FRAMES

However, they serve as a halfway house for many plants that are eventually to be grown outdoors, but which needed artificial warmth for germination or protection. If the glasshouse has been used to start off seeds in late winter and early to mid-spring, there will come a time when there is no more room for them indoors. A frame close to the glasshouse will supply this extra space and will provide suitable conditions for hardening off. If plants are not hardened off at the right time it can put paid to a summer display or a successful harvest.

During the summer, you can keep soft and half-ripe cuttings in a frame while they root. It provides protection, warmth at night, shade from the hot sun, and a humid atmosphere. You can germinate and grow annual seeds, sown in late spring or early summer in a frame, to provide a

flowering display in the cool glasshouse in winter, as with cineraria. Similarly, seeds sown in early autumn for a spring display in the cold house, such as sweetpeas, can be over-wintered safely in a frame.

Bulbs, corms and tubers which have flowered in winter or spring and then lie dormant through the summer because of drought conditions in their native countries can be put in a frame out of the way to rest and ripen, but keep an eye on them, as some have a habit of starting themselves into growth again. Cyclamen often do this, and it is easy to miss the signs of growth in the middle

Hardcore   Loam on compost

Above: *Three uses for frames:*
1 *Direct planting into compost or topsoil on a hardcore base, for crops, cuttings and pricking out; if possible the bed should extend beyond the frame.*

of the summer jobs, and then suddenly discover an elongated and thirsty plant.

Some perennial plants, which have flowered in spring, such as auriculas, primulas and many alpine plants, need shade and a cool root run in summer. The pots should be plunged up to the rim in moist peat in a frame, with the glass shaded but also well ventilated.

PREPARING FRAMES

Frames can be used for direct planting, for standing out containers of seedlings, cuttings and plants, or as a plunge-bed. The latter alternative is very useful, for instance, for bringing on bulbs such as hyacinths intended for Christmas flowering. If used for direct planting, the site for the frame should be dug out to a depth of about 12in (30cm). Put a thin layer of hardcore in the base of the hole, followed by a good quality loam or potting compost to fill it in. As a standing-out ground, the hardcore should be at a depth of 12in (30cm), with a layer of coarse ashes, or shingle on top, and a finer layer to finish off. Each layer should be rammed down. A quicker alternative is to replace the top layer of

soil with shingle, but this will develop into a muddy and moss-ridden surface in a year or two, if the seasons are wet. For both planting and standing-out, it is helpful to prepare the ground to an area slightly larger than that of the frame. For plunging plants, a depth of 7in (17cm) of peat should be added to a layer of shingle.

If the frame is to fulfil all three functions listed above, it will have to be partitioned into separate units.

SITING A FRAME

A suitable site for a frame is one that faces south and is sheltered from the north and east. If it is close to a wall or fence, allow ample space for walking behind it. If it is close to the glasshouse facilities can be shared, and it will be convenient for carrying containers. During late spring, summer and early autumn, it will need regular ventilation and, depending on the plants inside, it will need to be shaded, unless of the opaque type. In winter you will need mats, sacking or plastic sheeting to give protection against the cold at night. Soil-heating cables can be a useful accessory for this purpose.

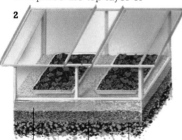

Fine ash   Coarse ashes   Hardcore

2 *As a standing-out area for boxes or pots of young plants needing to be hardened off before planting out, or protected from cold in autumn. The base material must be well drained.*

Peat in frame   Shingle

3 *As a plunge-bed, containing peat or coarse sand, for plants to be ripened in summer, such as bulbs, for overwintering bulbs for forcing or for tender plants, to keep the roots clear of frost.*

PLANTS FOR THE COLD GREENHOUSE

The cold house has no artificial heat in winter, but with insulation, the temperature should not drop more than a degree below freezing unless the weather is very severe. If prolonged hard frost does occur, you should wrap the pots of the following plants in some form of insulation; aspidistra, camellia, *Campanula isophylla,* chlorophytum, citrus, ceropegia, heptapleurum, hibiscus, lachenalia, pelargonium and sedum. You should also protect the top growth of the following at night: aspidistra, citrus, ceropegia, fatsia, hedera, heptapleurum, pelargonium, primula. Alternatively, you could put them temporarily in a frost-free room in the house.

Above: *Camellias are handsome evergreen shrubs: this one is* Camellia reticulata *'Willow Wand'.*

Above: *The pink flowers of nerines appear in September. This is* Nerine bowdenii, *also called the Guernsey Lily.*

Name
Aspidistra elatior (Parlour palm)
Asplenium scolopendrium (Hart's-tongue fern)
Camellia
Campanula isophylla (Italian bellflower)
Chlorophytum elatum 'Variegatum' (Spider plant)
Citrus (Orange, lemon)
Ceropegia woodsii (Hearts-entangled)
Fuchsia
Hedera helix (Ivy)
Heptapleurum arboricola (Parasol plant)
Hyacinthus (hyacinth)
Iris reticulata
Lachenalia tricolor (Cape cowslip)
Lathyrus odoratus (sweetpea)
Narcissus (daffodil, jonquil)
Nerine bowdenii
Pelargonium (geranium)
Primula auricula
Saxifraga stolonifera (Mother-of-thousands)
Sedum sieboldii

Type of plant/ Foliage	Flower colour/ Season	Height & spread
Herbaceous perennial Evergreen, glossy, leathery	Purple Late spring	20 x 20in (50 x 50cm)
Fern Evergreen, oblong	Foliage plant	6-18in x 12in (15-45cm x 30cm)
Shrub Evergreen, glossy	Pink, white, red March-April	5 x 4ft (1·5 x 1·2m) in tubs
Perennial trailer Evergreen	Blue, white July-October	trailing to 12-15in (30-38cm)
Herbaceous perennial Evergreen, green and white stripes	White July-September	18-36in (45 x 90cm)
Shrubby tree Evergreen	White March-April	48 x 36in (120 x 90cm) in tubs
Trailing corm Green, striped white	Pale purple June-October	trailing to 36in (90cm)
Shrub Almost evergreen	Purple, carmine, pink, white, orange All year if allowed	average 18-24in x 8-18in (45-60cm x 20-45cm)
Trailing Evergreen; green or variegated	Foliage plant	Trailing/climbing as space allows
Shrub Evergreen	Foliage plant	Up to 6 x 18ft (1·8 x 5m)
Bulb	Pink, white, blue, yellow, orange Christmas, March-April	6-9in x 5in (15-23cm x 12cm)
Bulb	Purple, blue January	4 x 2in (10 x 5cm)
Bulb Dark-spotted	Yellow and red March-April	9 x 4in (23 x 10cm)
Annual climber	All colours June-September	Climbing to 7 x 5ft (2·1 x 1·5m)
Bulb	Yellow, white, pink, orange February-April	4-18in x 2-4in (10-45cm x 5-10cm)
Bulb	Pink September	18in x 6in (45 x 15cm)
Herbaceous perennial More or less evergreen	Red, white, pink, magenta, purple, orange June-December	6-24in x 6-18in (15-60cm x 15-45cm)
Herbaceous perennial Evergreen	Blue, purple, yellow, reddish March-April	6-9in x 3-6in (15-23cm x 7·5-15cm)
Herbaceous perennial	White May	6 x 6in (15 x 15cm)
Herbaceous trailing Blue-grey	Purple September-October	Trailing to 12in (30cm)

PLANTS FOR THE COOL GREENHOUSE

In the cool greenhouse the temperature should not drop below 45°F (7°C) in winter, so some artificial heating is required, but not a great deal, and not necessarily during that time. All the plants listed on the previous two pages in the chart for the cold house can be grown in a cool house, too. As a result they will flower earlier.

Above: Achimenes 'Rose Red' is a good variety of the Hot Water Plant, so called because it prefers tepid to cold water.

Above: Passiflora caerulea racemosa is a fine variety of Passion Flower: a vigorous grower, it may need checking.

Name
Achimenes (hot-water plant)
Begonia, double-flowered
Begonia, semperflorens
Calceolaria
Cineraria
Cobaea scandens (cup-and-saucer plant)
Coleus (flame nettle)
Cyclamen
Heliotropium (heliotrope)
Hoya carnosa (wax flower)
Impatiens (busy Lizzie)
Lippia citriodora (lemon-scented verbena)
Mathiola (stocks)
Myrtus communis (myrtle)
Passiflora caerulea (passion-flower)
Plumbago capensis (Cape leadwort)
Salpiglossis
Schizanthus (butterfly flower)
Schlumbergera (Christmas cactus)
Sinningia (gloxinia)
Tradescantia albovittata (wandering Jew)
Zebrina pendula (purple wandering Jew)

Type of plant/ foliage	Flower colour/ season	Height & spread
Tuberous	All colours July-September	6-12in x 6-12in (15-30cm x 15-30cm)
Tuberous	Not blue or purple July-September	12-24in x 12-18in (30-60cm x 30-45cm)
Fibrous-rooted Green, wine-red	Pink, white, red July-November	8 x 8in (20 x 20cm)
Annual	Not blue/April-June	9 x 9in (23 x 23cm)
Annual	Not orange December-February	12 x 15in (30 x 38cm)
Annual climber	Purple and green July-October	10ft (3m) height
Annual All colours but blue	Blue August-October	18-30in x 10-12in (45-75cm x 25-30cm)
Tuberous White-marked, green leaves	Pink, white, magenta, wine December-January	6-12in x 6-12in (15-30cm x 15-30cm)
Shrubby	Purple, white, fragrant June-October	Up to 6 x 3ft (1·8m x 90cm)
Climber Evergreen	Pink and white June-September	10-12ft (3-3·6m) high
Annual to perennial Evergreen	All colours except blue All year	12-18in x 9-15in (30-45cm x 23-38cm)
Shrub Lemon-scented	Purple August	10-15ft x 5-7ft (3-4·5m x 1·5-2·1m)
Biennial	Purple, white, pink, cream, scented February-March	9-12in x 4in (23-30cm x 10cm)
Shrub Evergreen, aromatic	White May-August	To 10 x 4ft (3 x 1·2m)
Perennial	Blue, white and pink-purple June-September	Vigorous, to 25 x 6ft (7·5 x 1·8m)
Perennial climber	Blue June-September	10-15ft x 4ft (3-4·5m x 1·2m)
Annual	All colours July-September or March-April	24-30in x 6-8in (60-75cm x 15-20cm)
Annual	Not blue April-May or July-August	12-18in x 8-12in (30-45cm x 20-30cm)
Cactus Evergreen	Magenta December-January	8in x 30in (20cm x 75cm)
Tuberous	Red, white, pink blue, purple July-September	9 x 24in (23 x 60cm)
Trailing Evergreen, white striped	White June-September	Trailing, to 24in (60cm)
Trailing Evergreen, purple, green and white striped	Purplish June-September	Trailing 12-15in (30-38cm)

Tomatoes grown in the cold-house from seed should start to crop during midsummer. They may start two weeks earlier in mild districts, or two weeks later in more northern areas. The yield when grown on the cordon system should be at least 6lb (3kg) per plant.

You will need:
1 quarter-size seed-tray (for 12-24 plants).
2in (5cm) pots or 1 half-size seed tray.
3½in (9cm), 6in (15cm) and 9in (23cm) pots; it is possible to pot straight from 3½in (9cm) to 9in (23cm), but the plants do suffer a check.
Drainage material if clay pots are used.
Seed compost.
Potting compost (if JI, No 1 and 3)
7ft (2·1m) canes/stakes.
4-ply fillis; a heated propagator; liquid tomato fertilizer.
A source of artificial heat for night time in mid-late spring.
Work with warmed compost and water in the early stages, thereafter at atmospheric temperature unless this is markedly low.
Sowing: Sow seed singly ½in (1·3cm) apart at 60°F (16°C), cover with ¼in (6mm) sieved seed compost. Water and cover. Germination time: about 7 days.
Pricking out: Prick out as illustrated in J.I. No 1 potting compost, water and keep at 60°F (16°C) by night, 65°F (18°C) by day.
Potting: Pot successively two or three times into 3½-4in (9-10cm), 6in (15cm) and finally 9in (23cm) pots or into the border, when the first flower truss is opening. Water-in each time and keep temperature at 55-65°F (13-18°C). Space finally at 18in (45cm) x 2ft (60cm).
Support: Supply 1 cane per plant and tie tops of canes to wires running just below the roof. Water well before final planting and do not water again for 4-5 days; planting compost or soil

should be well soaked a day before planting.
Spraying: Spray plants, as illustrated, daily in the mornings to help pollination.
Sideshooting and tying: Twist the single stem round its support clockwise as it grows and tie it gently with fillis. Remove the sideshoots when tiny; take care not to remove growing tip of main shoot as it can easily be mistaken for sideshoot, if you are in a hurry.
Watering: Water regularly; never

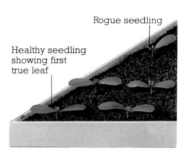

Above: *Tomato seeds are large enough to be sown spaced out, and thus have an excellent start; when the first true leaf shows they are ready for pricking out into 2in (5cm) pots or trays.*

Above: *Keep your tomatoes growing until the leaves are touching, or the roots fill the pot, and then pot them into 3½-4in (9-10cm) pots until the first flower truss shows; then plant out.*

Give plants a
light overhead
spray daily

Stop growth by
breaking off
growing tip
leaf above
the 6th truss

Pinch out
sideshoots
in the leaf
joints

Flower truss

Tie plants to
canes

Knuckle

Pick by bending
back at knuckle

allow plants to become dry.
When 6 fruit trusses are swelling,
each plant will need up to 1
gal (4·5 litres) of water daily
in hot weather.

Feeding: Start to feed with a
tomato fertilizer when the first
truss has set, as the manufacturer
directs.

Stopping: As shown in illustra-
tion; the plants will grow a
little taller after this.

Defoliating: Remove leaves
flush with the stem, to help
ripening, starting beneath and up
to the lowest ripening truss.

Picking: Pick as shown with the
calyx attached. Ripen at end of
season by putting in a warm
dark place.

Varieties: 'Big Boy' has large
fleshy fruit 3in-4in (7·5cm-10cm)
in diameter. A single fruit can
weigh 1lb (½kg). Allow 3 trusses
only per plant.
'Eurocross' ripens early and
produces a heavy crop. It is
resistant to leaf-mould.
'Grenadier' yields a large fruit.
It is resistant to leaf-mould and
stem-canker.
'Moneymaker' sets easily. The
fruit is a regular size.

Troubles: *Magnesium deficiency;*
yellowing between the main
veins of the leaves. Spray leaves
with a solution of Epsom salts
at 2oz (60g) to 1¼gal (5·5litre) of
water in a fine mist and repeat
at weekly intervals four times.
Leaf-mould (Cladosporium):
yellow spots on leaves, with grey
mould on the under-surface
in the area of the spots, spreading
rapidly in crowded, humid conditions. Use resistant varieties,
remove worst affected leaves,
increase air circulation, and spray
with systemic fungicide.
Blossom-end rot: grey to black,
hard dry patch on base of fruit,
opposite stalk end, due to check
in plant's water supply and
irregular watering generally.
Blotchy ripening: yellow or green
patches on fruit when ripe, as a
result of high temperatures when
the sun is shining on the fruit.

MELONS: COOL-HOUSE CULTIVATION

Melons can be grown and ripened out-doors in cool temperate climates with the help of a frame, but it depends on a warm late summer and autumn. You can start the plants with the help of artificial warmth in the early stages. The fruit will then form earlier, and so be able to take advantage of the maximum mid-summer warmth to ripen. The fruits grow from side stems. Usually four is the optimum number, but the Ogen variety can carry up to eight.

You will need:
A heated propagator.
2in (5cm) pots.
Drainage material if clay pots are used.
4in (10cm) pots.
Grow-bag(s) (2 plants per bag if not planting direct into the greenhouse border).
A source of artificial heat for night-time in mid-spring and early summer.
Seed compost.
Potting compost (if JI, No1).
Wires.
3-ply fillis.
Split canes.
Liquid fertilizer.
Rotted organic matter.
Work with warmed compost, as for tomatoes, and prepare the soil and wiring at the same time as you sow the seeds.
Soil preparation: Dig the soil a spade's depth and fork up the base. Mix well-rotted garden compost or similar material with the soil in the proportion of 1:5 by volume respectively Return to hole and form a mound.
Wiring: Use wire-mesh 8in (20cm) square and attach it to a wire running along the roof ridge and another 6in (15cm) above the soil, behind planting site. Use a horizontal wire in the middle running the length of the house to provide further support.
Sowing: Sow seeds as shown, cover and keep at 70°F (21°C). Sow more seed than you need,

as germination can be erratic. It takes 4-7 days.
Seedling care: Maintain a temperature of 60°F-65°F (16°C-18°C) and water as required. Seedlings should be ready to pot-on in 7 to 10 days.
Potting: When the roots have filled the pot or the first true leaf shows, whichever is first, move the young plants into 4in (10cm) pots of potting compost. Water them in, and continue with the same temperature.
Stopping: Stop as shown: retain the two strongest side-shoots.
Planting: Plant out about 3 weeks later, either 18in (45cm) apart on a ridge, in the greenhouse border, or in grow-bags, 2 plants per bag, spaced evenly. Support

2" (5cm) pots
Moist seed compost

Top: *Melon seeds are sown singly in 2in (5cm) pots, placed on edge, about ½in (13mm) deep, at 60-70°F (16-21°C).*

Above: *Pinch out the growing tip above the 4th leaf.*

and water the plants in. Maintain at least 55°F (13°C) at night.

Training: As the plants grow, attach the 2 main stems of each plant and the developing side-shoots to the wires, spacing them evenly. Stop the sub-sideshoots one leaf beyond the female flower, and stop the main stems when they reach the roof.

Pollination: Use a cheap paintbrush to dust pollen onto the centre of the female flower. When setting is well under way, and some fruits have started to swell, remove all but four well-spaced fruits.

Watering: Keep the plants well-watered. They need a good deal of water, especially while the fruit is swelling.

Feeding: If the soil in the border is poor, or the plants are in grow-bags, start to feed them about a month after planting with a potash-high liquid fertilizer.

Harvesting: Reduce watering and stop feeding when the swelling stops and hair-line cracks start to appear around the stalk, where it is attached to the fruit. Harvest the fruit as soon as the cracks deepen.

Varieties: 'Hero of Lockinge' small, white flesh, good flavour; 'Sweetheart', cantaloupe-type, medium, orange flesh, green skin; 'Ogen', small, 4½in (11cm) wide, very good flavour, yellow-green flesh, green striped skin.

Troubles: red spider mite and collar rot.

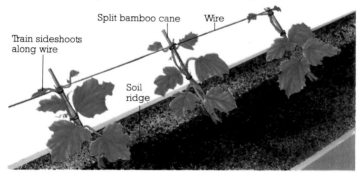

Train sideshoots along wire

Split bamboo cane

Wire

Soil ridge

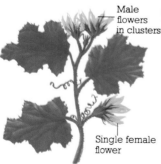

Male flowers in clusters

Single female flower

Top: *Melons are put into their permanent sites in late spring, on a mound or ridge, with a split cane directed towards the support wiring, up which the main sideshoots are trained.*

Above left: *Female flowers have a small round growth behind the flower, the future melon; male flowers have narrow stems.*

Above: *Swelling melons need support in nets or slings.*

INDEX

PICTURE CREDITS

Artists
Copyright of the illustrations on the pages following
the artists' names is the property of Salamander Books Ltd.
Janos Marffy: 18, 19, 28, 30-31, 33, 41, 42-43, 58, 67, 72, 73, 74, 75
Colin Newman (Linden Artists): Front cover

Photographs
The publishers wish to thank the following photographers
who have supplied photographs for this book. The photographs
have been credited by page number and position on the page:
B (Bottom), T (Top), BL (Bottom Left), etc.
Eric Crichton: Endpapers, 12, 14, 15, 16, 17, 20, 21, 22, 23, 24, 25, 27,
31, 34, 35, 37, 38, 39, 41, 44, 45, 46, 48, 49, 50, 51, 52, 53, 54, 55, 56, 57, 59,
61, 62, 63, 68, 70, Back cover
Tania Midgley: Title page, 6, 9, 10, 13, 26